# BEFRIENDING MY BRAIN

## A Psychosis Story

# BEFRIENDING MY BRAIN

## A Psychosis Story

### James Lindsay

Cherish
EDITIONS

First published in Great Britain 2023 by Cherish Editions

Cherish Editions is a trading style of Shaw Callaghan Ltd & Shaw Callaghan 23 USA, INC.

The Foundation Centre

Navigation House, 48 Millgate, Newark

Nottinghamshire NG24 4TS UK

www.triggerhub.org

Text Copyright © 2023 James Lindsay

British Library Cataloguing in Publication Data

A CIP catalogue record for this book is available upon request from the British Library

ISBN: 978-1-913615-94-9

This book is also available in the following eBook formats:

ePUB: 978-1-913615-95-6

James Lindsay has asserted his right under the Copyright, Design and Patents Act 1988 to be identified as the author of this work

Cover design by More Visual

Typeset by Lapiz Digital Services

I want to dedicate this book to anyone who is going through (or has been through) a mental health struggle. I hope you are reading from a good place, but if not, I really hope my book helps you along your way.

Please take my word for it: it does and will get better. If you're struggling right now, I can appreciate how things can feel bleak, and the feeling seems permanent. I want you to not only work on getting better for yourself as you are now, but also do it for the version of yourself in the future, who is incredibly proud of you for taking steps in the right direction, even if they are small steps.

Recovery is always possible, and hope is never far away.

# CONTENTS

# CHAPTER 1

# LIFE BEFORE PSYCHOSIS

According to the mental health charity Mind, psychosis (also called a psychotic experience or psychotic episode) is when you perceive or interpret reality in a very different way from people around you. You might also be said to "lose touch" with reality. When I was 26, I had no idea what psychosis was; I didn't even have a good knowledge of mental illness in general. I knew a bit about anxiety, as I had suffered from it as a child, teenager and still sometimes in small doses as an adult. Little did I know, mental illness was about to become a big part of my life. Before I can talk in detail about my psychotic episode, though, I want to explain my background and the circumstances that led up to it.

As I mentioned, anxiety had introduced itself to me at an early age, and it decided to stick around and follow me like a stray dog. I was sprinting away from it like Crash Bandicoot running from a boulder – yes, I'm a 90s kid and a proud nerdy gamer for life. However, with mental illness, you can try avoiding it, you can try fighting it, you can try ignoring it and hoping it will go away (don't do that), but ultimately it can sneak up on you when you least expect it. Looking back now, it is clear that my breakdown built up over time as my anxiety increased, but psychosis still gut-punched me hard to finish me off. In boxing terms, anxiety hit me with steady jabs and hooks, but psychosis landed the knockout blow.

I have always been a worrier. I was told many times by family and friends growing up, "You worry too much." I remember this started in my school days when I went to a decent public secondary school in St

Albans – quite an affluent area when you're from Watford like I am. I wasn't bullied or picked on more than the average boy, but I took what people said very seriously, and I wasn't always good at taking a joke. My daily thought process would involve going over every lesson I had that day, which kids I might encounter and what they might possibly say about me. I was basically worrying about things before they even happened, giving myself stress over nothing, which I now know is called catastrophising. If someone did make a comment that I didn't like, it would ruin my day and destroy my confidence. This would then feed into the thought process for the next day and make it worse. One morning, I was in floods of tears and shouting at my parents, refusing to go to school because I couldn't bear the thought of having a bad day. Sometimes at school, I would go to reception and tell the lady there that I was having a panic attack, and she needed to call my mum to take me home, which was completely made up. This was all over the threat of name-calling from other kids, rather than physical abuse. I might sound like a right little wimp of a kid to some, but in reality, I think these are more common behaviours of kids than you might think, and they show the power of the mind at a young age. This is why I believe that mental health and well-being should be prioritised as early as childhood.

My school reports and teacher feedback comments were mainly positive. I went through some of them that Mum has kept, and there are recurring comments like "polite", "hard-working" and even "pleasure to teach". There were also things said that summed up my lack of confidence and hinted at my anxiety. I think that this snippet from my year 8 progress report, describing my performance in drama class, reflected me pretty well:

*James is a very quiet member of the class. He can struggle working in a group and prefers to take a back seat and allow others to dominate the group instead. His effort is good in most classes, and he clearly enjoys some aspects of drama. However, I would like to see him take more of a positive role within the group.*

*Teacher: Mr White      24/06/2003*

I want to share another example of my anxious young mind when I was around seven years old. One evening I was happily eating a McDonald's Happy Meal with my mum, auntie and cousin. This utter delight of mine was ruined, however, when I started choking on my burger. I had got food stuck like this before from ravenously eating without chewing, but this was a particularly scary experience. Mum was pushing in my stomach to try and get the bloody burger out, and it was causing quite a scene. Finally, I gave up trying to cough it out and managed to swallow it, but before I did this, I literally thought I was going to die – and can you imagine the headline in the *Watford Observer* that some kid choked to death on a Happy Meal? This experience affected me so badly that I was terrified of eating food that was any effort to chew. Baked beans and soup became my new favourites – thank God for beans and soup. I would refuse to have any meal without a drink nearby in case of an emergency. This became an issue when I went on the year 8 school trip to Disneyland Paris. I broke down in tears before getting on the coach, and Mum had to explain to my favourite science teacher, Mr Moakes (an absolute legend), that I had this "swallowing problem". When I eventually got on the coach, I wore sunglasses (on a dark, cloudy day) to hide that I had been crying.

By the time I progressed to year 10 to start GCSEs, my anxiety that started years earlier seemed to be advancing at an even faster rate. Most people get called a name that they hate at some point, right? This was my time. Do you remember watching the very first *Shrek* film? The villain character in that is called Lord Farquaad, a tiny white man with long black hair. Well, once that film came out, some git in my year thought they had made a great comparison by calling me "Lord Farquaad". I was definitely a small kid at that point, and my growth spurt was nowhere to be seen (despite me drinking copious amounts of orange juice and milk because I heard somewhere it could help). They were spot on with the height, but back then, I had a mini afro! So, I thought I looked nothing like this twit in the film and didn't like the label at all. Of course, if kids see you don't like it, it gets worse. Within a week, I was walking down the corridor to my lessons, and people were pointing and shouting, "LORD FARQUAAAAAAAD, HE HOOOOFED, AND HE POOOOOFED, AND HE SIGNED AN EVICTION NOTICE!" (If you've seen the film, you know this is one of its many great quotes).

Looking back, I actually think, *Bravo, guys*. It was genuinely a good joke, and it got very popular around school – not just in my year, either. Once, when I was walking my dog at the weekend, two older boys walked past me and looked at me. They let me walk away, but I heard in the distance behind me, "LORD FARQUAAAAD!" I was sort of famous around school, I guess – if only my anxiety had let me take a joke back then. I should have embraced it and took the piss out of myself like I do now. I'm not having a go at anyone who called me this; in fact, if we have a big school reunion, I might go in fancy dress as Farquaad himself! Sadly, though, young me couldn't cope with this, and I did something a bit lame. After an English class during my A-Levels – the joke was still going strong three years later – I admitted to my teacher that I didn't like it. The next lesson, I was shocked when she announced to the class that she wanted to see four girls sitting at the front at the end of class. In another lesson that week, one of those girls who used to call me Lord, said, "Could you pass me that calculator please, James?" with a warm smile. I was so surprised to hear my actual name, it took me a while to process what she wanted! Word must have got round that they weren't allowed to call me that anymore. It made the rest of school more bearable, but it also shows that my fellow pupils were just trying to have a laugh with me. I could've won an early duel with anxiety by just opening up more and talking to people.

School was also full of great times. Of course, I loved playing football with mates at lunchtime, and I did manage to enjoy things like that Paris trip. I had realised that I was definitely an overthinker. This did have benefits, though, and I think it helped me get decent GCSEs. By the time sixth form came around, I had built some confidence. However, when it came to new teenage experiences, like attempting to get girls to like me, having a fun social life and trying new things like alcohol, anxiety would rear its ugly head and say, "Remember me? I'm not finished with you yet — not even close."

Looking back on these times, my anxiety seemed to have adapted like a virus. I had somewhat overcome the silly overthinking of possible disasters that used to be a daily routine, but my brain would then decide to create a new problem. I remember my loved ones used to say to me, "You don't seem happy unless you've got something to worry about". This was true — as soon as I stopped being concerned about one thing, my mind would automatically throw something else in its place. This was precisely when social anxiety decided to take centre stage.

I had always been a social kid who loved the company of others, choosing to surround myself with friends. But starting from young adulthood around age 17, up until my early to mid-20s, I have at times been nervous by the prospect of socialising with others. In sixth form, I thought I had found a solution for this: alcohol. I remember going to parties and not feeling comfortable with talking to friends — unless I got absolutely off my face on beer and Jägerbombs. I was one of those quiet ones who came alive after a drink, and people loved this. "You're so funny when you're drunk," I would be told, so I think I ended up trying to use this "constructive feedback" by doing what I thought they wanted and trying to fit in. Of course, this led to me embarrassing myself on more than one occasion, and there are many funny stories. For my 18th birthday, I was so wasted that I passed out while standing up on the dancefloor, collapsing to the floor of a nightclub in Watford called Area, although it has a new name now. I had to be carried out of the club, and I think there is still a video on Facebook somewhere of me being revived on my mate's lap and talking utter nonsense. Luckily, I had good friends who promptly delivered me back home to Mum. I passed out on the sofa in the lounge and woke up around 7am, my clothes and our nice sofa covered in vomit. This was to be the first of many drunken stories — most of which still make me laugh, to be fair — but, in hindsight, I didn't need booze to enjoy any of these wonderful moments.

Interestingly, even though it would be nearly ten years until my anxiety introduced me to its best friend – another evil villain that goes by the name of psychosis – I was given an exclusive sneak preview of my future mental illness. It was almost like a trailer for the movie called *Jim Loses His Mind*. For my English Literature A-Level, we read and studied *One Flew Over the Cuckoo's Nest*, and we watched the superb Oscar-winning film adaption starring the legendary Jack Nicholson. I was fascinated by this book, and I really enjoyed learning about mental illnesses. Never in a million years did I think I would almost become one of the characters when I got sectioned.

In and out of the classroom, my shyness, awkwardness and anxiety gradually reduced, thanks in part to my first part-time job at Sainsbury's in Watford. There, I had to talk to customers on the checkout, and this slowly improved my confidence and conversational skills, despite encountering some unpleasant customers – although I now write that off as character building. I was able to keep this job and get decent A-Level results.

By the time I moved down to Portsmouth for university, I was ready to make further progress. There were new challenges, though, such as living away from home with new people and being independent. Surprisingly, I think I took this all in my stride. University was a brilliant experience for me, and I became a new person – in a good way. I went there a boy and became somewhat of a man, I guess. I was still quite shy and awkward at the beginning, but I gained loads of confidence, and this was mainly due to meeting incredibly fun, supportive friends. I felt comfortable talking to them about anything. We really clicked as a group and have some unbelievably good memories together. Anxiety was still hovering around, but I was able to keep it at bay.

The main problem I had with myself at this age was actually with the way that I looked. I had really bad acne on my face and I hated it. It got so bad that it gave me quite low confidence and self-esteem. I really wanted a girlfriend and to lose my virginity at this point, but acne gave me zero self-belief. I was given so many different creams and ointments by doctors, but none of them worked. Finally, in my second year, they prescribed me with a powerful drug called Roaccutane. It took a few months, but my skin finally started to clear up. As a result, I started to feel a bit better with how I looked.

My degree was in business administration, and when I graduated, I decided to do a master's in marketing, as this was my favourite subject out of everything we studied as undergraduates. I could've stayed in Portsmouth for the master's, but I decided to do it at the University of Hertfordshire, partly because the campus was a 20-minute drive from Watford, so I could live back at home with family. One of the reasons I wanted to do this is something that I haven't mentioned yet, something that happened during my glorious years in Pompey that was the complete opposite of glorious. It was early December in my second year (2009), and we were all due to go home for Christmas in a week. I was happily playing *Call of Duty* on my PlayStation 3 (I had moved on from *Crash Bandicoot*), when I got a surprise call from my auntie. I was initially delighted to hear from her and intrigued as to why she had called me, which quickly turned to concern when I heard the tone of her voice. "James," she said, "I'm so sorry to tell you this, but your mum and I are at Watford General Hospital. Your dad suffered a stroke this morning and he is currently in intensive care. Uncle Russell is happy to drive to Portsmouth tonight to come and get you, but would you rather take the train?"

This took a while to sink in, but when it did, it hit me like that train my auntie mentioned. So, I took up the offer of a lift, as I was in such a state that I couldn't face public transport. My dad, my hero who was responsible for some of the happiest moments of my life so far, could die and be gone forever. I tried my best to pack a suitcase while in floods of tears, told my shocked housemates that I was going home early and made the two-hour journey to the hospital. The following weeks were by far the scariest I had faced so far. Dad had to have a procedure carried out on his brain where the haemorrhage had occurred. At one point during those weeks, I remember being on the phone to a doctor who calmly explained to me that one of the risks of this procedure was death.

I am still so grateful that Dad made it through. The man to thank was a highly skilled surgeon who was able to cover up the haemorrhage area with a type of glue that will prevent it from happening again. I can't begin to comprehend this stuff, but it is incredible what medical professionals can do these days. And thank God we have the NHS in the UK, where the staff literally performs miracles like this on a weekly basis. Considering how bad someone can get even if they live after a stroke, Dad did remarkably well. He could still talk and had use of his body. I think that my brother Mark, my mum and I handled the situation well too. However, this is the type of traumatic event that can affect mental health. I was still a worrier despite my progress, but now I was concerned with looking after Dad, and I wanted to be there for my family, so this was part of why I wanted to do my master's at home. I also thought that I could concentrate better at home, where there were less distractions. It's amazing how an experience like this puts it all in perspective. At one time, I was worrying about the acne on my face and how disgusting I thought I looked, but I quickly forgot about all that when Dad gave us real cause for concern. It made my previous worries look a bit ridiculous by comparison.

I could waffle on about my time at Herts Uni and living back at home, but I don't think it's as relevant for this book, as the whole thing ended up going rather smoothly, and I managed to work hard and get a distinction. My next step was to do a ski season in Austria for six months. Again, I could tell you about my endless *piste* and off-*piste* skiing and snowboarding lessons around the beautiful snowy Alps, but this was another time when I was too busy having fun to let anxiety ruin it all. Anxiety didn't let this slide, though – pardon the pun. Once I returned to England to try and start building a successful career and finally find a girlfriend, it came back with a vengeance.

Since this chapter has covered my time at university, I thought it would be good to include a shortened version of the blog that I wrote in 2018 for Trigger Publishing, which contained loads of mental health advice for students.

# MENTAL HEALTH AT UNIVERSITY

My time at university was incredible, and I have so many happy memories, but back then, my knowledge of mental health was limited. I wish I knew then what I've learnt in my 20s about maintaining good mental well-being.

I think it's important to surround yourself with people with whom you can talk to about the serious stuff and have good banter too. A great way to "find your tribe" is by getting involved with clubs and societies, in addition to making friends from your course, halls of residence, etc.

I joined the Ski & Snowboarding Club in my first year, but was surprised that I only got along with one person from the group, since I love skiing. This was okay, though, as my best friends at uni were from my halls. We ended up joining the Tennis & Badminton Club in third year and had some amazing nights out with them – and, of course, the occasional sessions of hopelessly swinging a racket!

You might not get along with everyone, but if you're putting yourself out there enough, then you've got the best chance of finding a nice, supportive group of friends, who you can talk to about anything.

Uni is full of fun and exciting experiences, but you might also experience stress from things like assignments, exams, relationships, friendships, living away from home – the list goes on! Even if you're not sporty, there are loads of options out there – your uni might be running something that suits you.

Apart from keeping active, I would also encourage anyone going to uni or currently experiencing it to make sure you communicate and be open with your closest mates about anything that is worrying you. I've always been a massive worrier, and I was not always as open and honest with people during uni as I am with them now. Men in particular are not as good at talking about feelings, but once you're brave enough to take that first step, you'll be amazed at how much better you feel after talking with a friend. They are probably experiencing something similar and will be relieved that you shared with them – not to mention proud of you!

Two friends spoke to me separately about their anxiety and panic attacks, and we talked about the medication and counselling that they had received. I feel even closer to them now, and we are very strong and supportive together as a group. If you can find this while at uni, I guarantee you will feel so much better, and you will be able to concentrate more on what makes you happy!

I should also cover the subject of social media. I have always loved social media and I use it regularly in my job and personal life, but I've also seen the negative effects it can have. We very much live in the digital age now, where you can see snapshots of everyone's lives using Facebook, Instagram, Twitter, LinkedIn and so on. I wish I realised back at uni that this is often a "highlight reel", and people only post what they want you to see. In reality, their lives might not be as glamorous, and we all have tougher times that we won't necessarily publish. These days, if something annoys me on one of these apps, I simply hit "unfollow" or "mute", which makes me feel loads better! As with friends in real life, you might be better off following only those on social media who make you happy and feel good.

Lastly, you can boost your mental well-being even further by eating and drinking well. Now, I know some nights you will want to treat yourself to a burger and chips, followed by drinking pints at the Student Union, showing off those dance moves in a club and maybe even getting a cheeky kebab before passing out in bed. There's absolutely nothing wrong with that – I used to do it regularly! But a sensible diet outside of that will do wonders for your mind. Fruit and veg will make you feel good and give you more energy to concentrate in those lectures, protein will help you recover from playing for your sports team, and the right carbs will keep you full and energised throughout the day. Uni is a fantastic opportunity to get into cooking, which becomes very therapeutic and rewarding the more you do it.

Thank you for reading, and remember to have fun and make the most of uni – that time can be some of the best years of your life!

# CHAPTER 2

# WHAT LED ME TO DEVELOP PSYCHOSIS

I met my first "proper serious" girlfriend in August 2013, through quite a common method these days: a dating website. I won't reveal her name for obvious reasons, so let's just call her Ellie. (At the time of writing, I don't know anyone named Ellie.) We clicked straight away and dated for around three months before having the "so, where is this going?" conversation. It was then that we decided to be boyfriend and girlfriend (cringe/giggle). I was so happy because she was beautiful and a good match for me in terms of personality and sense of humour. I'd had a brief relationship during my third year at Portsmouth, but it only lasted around two months – this one with Ellie was the real thing. Our first year as a couple was full of so many fond memories. We were very much in love and had some wonderful times together, including a trip to Bath and our first holiday together in sunny Tenerife.

When I met Ellie, I was working for a market research agency in St Albans, near where I lived with my parents and brother in Abbots Langley near Watford, Hertfordshire. She was a primary school teacher living with her friend from work in a town called Ware, also in Hertfordshire. (It's pronounced the same as "where" – don't make that joke, I've heard it hundreds of times.) I am mentioning my work situation because I believe the stress it gradually caused me was another factor in my eventual mental breakdown. Remember how I said anxiety had come back with a bang? It thrived off my work and relationship situations.

After about one year with Ellie, the main issue that caused our eventual break-up started to affect us. It is quite a personal and sensitive subject, so I won't go into too much detail about the situation, but it did have a massive impact on our relationship.

It also had a negative effect on our mental health. Ellie and I felt guilty that we had lost the spark. I felt bad that I was not able to overcome this and very frustrated that I could not fix it, which wasn't good for my confidence and self-esteem or hers, either. I suggested we see a doctor, which Ellie was not keen on due to embarrassment. This caused some of our first conflict and arguments as a couple, which was unheard of before then.

Eventually, we did see a doctor, who did not turn out to be helpful, as they just suggested things to try that we had already attempted. Ellie had also been taking the pill, but the doctor did not see this as part of the issue. Our next step was to visit a clinic to see if they could help us. They carried out various tests on both of us, but they didn't find anything wrong with me or her, and I remember being annoyed that their eventual conclusion was essentially the same as what the doctor had suggested before. It felt like such a dead end.

By this point, we were living together too. Her previous flatmate had moved out to live with her new boyfriend, so I moved out of my family home to live in Ware with Ellie. I have very warm memories of this point in my life, despite our problems. I think our strong love for each other is what made the relationship last as long as it did (three years), whereas some couples might have given up sooner. I was determined to overcome this because I knew that, apart from this issue, we had a near-perfect relationship, but I wasn't prepared for us to be a platonic couple for the rest of our lives.

Eventually, we went back to the doctor again, and she recommended therapy. We started sessions with a local company that offered various types of relationship support. I think we had around ten sessions in total with mixed results. Ellie wasn't keen on talking to our therapist, who was an older woman. It became clear she was very uncomfortable discussing the situation with her.

She also admitted to me around this time that she thought she was experiencing mild depression. I was starting to become increasingly affected by my old enemy, anxiety. I think the whole experience was not good for our self-esteem.

I want to introduce a new perspective at this point. It is good to get other viewpoints because I can't actually remember some of what happened to me, due to a very poorly mind. This chat is with my good friend, Tommy. We went to uni together in Portsmouth, but he lives in Shrewsbury, which is 140 miles from Watford, so we have a long-distance bromance. He was beyond supportive during my hard times, so I spoke to him about the early beginnings of my eventual breakdown.

## CONVERSATION WITH – TOMMY

**James:** "So, what are your first memories of where it all started to go downhill for me?"

**Tommy:** "I remember one conversation we had at the time. I had just got home from sailing club on a Sunday afternoon. You were going for a walk, but were annoyed because Ellie was supposed to come with you and changed her mind at the last second, just as you were walking out the front door."

**James:** "Okay, I think I wanted to talk about our problems during the walk. There was a lovely, quiet route along a river, near where we were living. I hate staying inside all day, as you well know!"

**Tommy:** "Exactly, so you ended up walking alone instead and calling me to have a rant. This ended up being a regular occurrence. I didn't see it as abnormal behaviour, though; I would've done the same thing in your position. Having an agony aunt like me is a good way to de-stress!"

**James:** "Absolutely. I was keen for us to talk about the situation and work on getting it better. She wanted this too, but she was much shyer and more embarrassed about it than me, even when we found out it is a common relationship issue. So, how many times was I phoning you to have a moan?"

**Tommy:** "Hmm, a handful. It went on for a while. We speak regularly over the phone and Skype anyway, so it just sometimes became a small part of the conversation. As the months (and years) went on, though, I think it slowly evolved and became a bigger part of the conversation."

**James:** "It's good that we were talking about it, and I'm thankful I have supportive friends like you to help. Ellie and I were obviously communicating regularly about it as well. I just wish she used her close friends to help her too, rather than hiding it from them. I think they could've made a big difference."

**Tommy:** "I couldn't agree more. Our conversations were not just you blowing off steam, they were constructive. We would come up with ideas together of ways you could help improve the situation, as you didn't want to give up on the relationship."

**James:** "Yes, I can't imagine how much worse it would've been without your help."

**James:** "So, eventually, I guess these conversations must have started to raise your alarm bells when I started to become mentally unwell. I think that was around the time I was breaking up with her, or was it before or after?"

**Tommy:** "It must've been before. It's hard to remember to be honest. However, what I do remember clearly, and I don't know if you know this, but the rest of the boys and I created a separate WhatsApp group from our main group, because we were all concerned about you."

**James:** "That doesn't surprise me. I kind of assumed that's what happened."

**Tommy:** "Yes, because you had called me and some of the other guys separately, each call sounding odd. We spoke to each other and agreed something wasn't right. Perhaps that was after you had the break-up, but before you went to the hospital."

Tommy definitely helped fill in the gaps, not just about this period, but several months after it when I was really in trouble. He even called the psychiatric ward where I was staying and spoke to me.

But back to Ellie and the lead-up to the illness. On top of the relationship situation, I was also putting myself under immense stress at work. My career in market research was not going how I wanted it to. I had started in an entry-level position for a large organisation in London, and I was frustrated that colleagues around me were getting promotions and pay rises, but I wasn't.

I didn't make it easier for myself by comparing my situation with friends. We live in the digital age of social media, where you can see snapshots of everyone's lives using Facebook, Instagram, Twitter and LinkedIn. I was getting too sucked into this and falling into the trap of seeing that someone my age or younger from school or university had updated their LinkedIn profile with a promotion, or posted a picture of their keys for a new home on Instagram, or a shared a photo of their engagement ring with an updated relationship status on Facebook.

It would really get me down and, in hindsight, I wish I could've just not worried about any of it. I wish I realised back then that social media is, as I said previously, a "highlight reel", and people only post what they want you to see. Their lives might not be as glamorous as they present them to be, and we all have tougher times that we won't necessarily post online. On top of that, it angered me that I wasn't using my marketing degree in my current job. All this, combined with frequent problems with Ellie, was making me a very stressed and unhappy man – but my anxiety was having a lovely old time with it all. I was constantly on the phone with Mum or one of my best friends, trying to find solutions to my worries. I was determined that we were going to get through it, and I didn't want to give up.

In total, our problem affected about two years of the relationship. When the therapy wasn't working, I told Ellie that I thought we needed to go on a break. This was so painful and broke my heart, but I realised at this point that I wasn't in a good way mentally and needed some space.

Our break only lasted about a week in the end, and things started to improve after we got back together – at first, anyway. However, after a few months, we were having the same old issues again, and I had to make one of the hardest decisions of my life at the time. I didn't want to break up with such an amazing person, but I knew deep down that I couldn't carry on living like this. Ellie had previously talked about us buying a property together – we were renting at the time – but I couldn't make that commitment when we had such a big problem.

I remember a few weeks before the break-up, we went on holiday for a week in Devon. By this point, I was pretty much convinced that there was no hope for us, but I decided I should use the trip as one last chance to see if we could somehow make it work. Surely we would be able to have some enjoyable moments together on holiday, where we had a nice little cottage to ourselves, away from the stresses of everyday life?

We tried, but as the week went on, I knew it wasn't going to be. I knew that if we couldn't succeed there, what chance would we have back home, where we had even less time and opportunities to be together? I did enjoy our time in Devon overall, but it was horrible knowing the whole time that I would have to have that horrific experience of ending it when we were back home.

Throughout those difficult two years, I was having frequent conversations with my close friends and my parents, seeking advice on what to do about the situation, as well as keeping them updated, as they were understandably concerned about us. I wouldn't tell Ellie about this because she didn't want anyone to know about our problem and was embarrassed, but I knew I couldn't go through this experience by myself.

We were, of course, talking to each other as a couple as well, and I think our communication did improve as a result. However, I don't think she actually shared our issues with her close friends and family until we had nearly reached the end of the relationship, which is a shame, as I think they could've helped and supported her in the same way my loved ones did for me.

I will never forget the evening where I sat down with Ellie on the sofa in our flat and ended our relationship. So many tears were shed from both of us. I had never seen her so sad and upset and I felt terrible. Her mum owned the flat that we were renting, so I immediately moved out and went to live with my parents and brother. It was crazy having to move all my stuff from the flat back to Watford. It felt like a backwards step at the time, but I knew I had no choice. It was not long after this that my breakdown began.

# CHAPTER 3

# MY WORLD BEGINS TO FALL APART

I had only been back living with my family for about a week when my health started to deteriorate. The amount of sleep I was getting every night fell dramatically. I would barely be getting an hour or two of sleep – some nights I would not sleep at all. I remember my mind was not able to switch off. Instead, it was in overdrive, filled with worries about what happened with Ellie and where it all went wrong. I also had many thoughts about the future, including finding a flat of my own and trying to embrace single life after two years without intimacy. The absence of sleep made me very alert and hyper – all I wanted to do was start this new chapter of my life and I couldn't relax. I took for granted back then how important sleep can be for mental health, and I think if I had known this, I might not have had such a setback.

Around this time, I ended up going to a barbecue in Basingstoke, hosted by Dan, one of my best friends from uni. He had a fantastic turnout, and pretty much the entire gang was there with their partners. Unfortunately, it was around the time that I was very sleep-deprived and starting to behave strangely. I remember getting the tube to London to get the train from Waterloo to Basingstoke. I was meant to be meeting a friend in London somewhere, and we were going to get the train together. He ended up driving there, but before I knew this, I decided to buy him a panini from Costa, as I was getting my own lunch. When I found out he wouldn't need it, I made a couple of very weird and random attempts to get rid of it, which make me cringe thinking back on them now. I got chatting to a girl opposite me on the tube and, at one point, I ended up offering her the panini. I can't imagine what must have been going through her mind as this random bloke she didn't know offered her food – what was I thinking!? She obviously said, "No thanks," and was very polite about it. I decided after that, as I was walking to Waterloo, that I would give it to a homeless person on the street, but I never saw one. I ended up going into some pub and asking them to just offer it to one of their customers, and I still remember the look of utter disbelief on their faces as I walked away. I wish I could say the odd behaviour stopped there.

I accidentally got a slow train to Basingstoke, which stopped at every station along the way and made me late to the barbecue. When I got there, I think I was the last one to arrive by quite some time. Dan was chatting to me in the hallway, and I turned around to see all my friends in his living room. Normally, I would be delighted to see everyone, but I was so stressed and sleep-deprived that all I wanted to do was burst into tears. I held it together and went to the kitchen with a couple of friends, rather than going to the room full of people. The others slowly started to filter into the kitchen, and I had calmed down by this point. They all just really wanted to see me and check I was okay after the break-up. The rest of the barbecue was mostly fine, but many of my friends could tell there was something wrong with me. Most of them left after a few hours, and then the four of us that were remaining decided to go on a night out in Basingstoke. I'm extremely ashamed to admit this part, but all I wanted to do at the time was hit on girls, which was not nice of me and not fair to Ellie, as I wouldn't have liked the idea of her doing the same. The morning after, my hangover was joined by a strong feeling of guilt. I was a complete mess, and it wasn't about to get any better.

Back home, according to my mum, I was constantly talking, jumping from one subject to another without making much sense. She would often get out of bed in the middle of the night and come and find me, and we would have long talks. I also started to experience bizarre and unusual thoughts in my head. One of the peculiar thoughts was that I was being headhunted by a company for a job, which definitely never happened – it was just an idea in my head that I had convinced myself was true. I remember a few months earlier, I had been for an interview for a job in programmatic advertising, which is where companies use the internet to track users' behaviour and then provide targeted adverts. Learning about this for the interview made me very aware that organisations could effectively follow me online, so I became a bit paranoid. I think that this knowledge, mixed with lack of sleep and the beginnings of psychosis, is why I believed that I was being headhunted.

Similarly, I also became convinced that my brother Mark was plotting against me (and reading this now seems so unbelievably ridiculous, as I know he would never do such a thing).

Since moving back home, I had decided that I was going to spend as much time as possible with him, which started off as a good thing, as we never used to hang out much. I took a greater interest in his life, including his plans to grow the YouTube channel he had started that was beginning to gain many subscribers. I genuinely wanted to help him out with this, as well as other big brother stuff, like helping him with his dating life. However, I took it too far and didn't give him space, and when he started to turn down my advice (which I don't blame him for, looking back), I didn't take this well. Somehow, I got it into my head that he had a motive against me, and it got so bad that I actually thought he was dangerous. I feel horrible thinking back about this because he is the loveliest and most caring guy you could ever meet. My parents even had to make him stay in his room in the lead-up to me being sectioned so that I couldn't see him.

The other strange behaviour of mine that I recall was writing on the furniture in my room. I think I thought I had to label everything that was mine for some reason. I also rearranged some of my bedroom, and this included some odd choices. I washed out an old plastic set of drawers from the garage, which is okay behaviour on its own. But then, during one of my sleepless nights, I decided to fill one of the drawers with spiders that I caught and put a label on the drawer that said, "Caution: Live Spiders". This is the last thing I would normally do in the middle of the night – or at any time of the day, for that matter. I was so bored and fed up with not being able to sleep that my mind was coming up with all sorts of crazy ideas.

During the daytime, I was watching TV and listening to the radio. However, I became convinced that I was receiving messages through both of these channels, telling me to do things like go on the internet and send someone a message by email or over social media. The lack of sleep and psychosis were messing up my mind massively – I was all over the place. At one point, I even thought the weather was speaking to me. The sun kept going behind clouds and reappearing, and I thought the timing of this was connected to what I was doing at the time. So, say I would come up with a new idea as the sun came out. That would make me think the idea was incredible. And when the sun went behind clouds and the room became darker, I would suddenly get a sense of deep dread and start worrying.

It didn't take Mum long to suggest that I needed to urgently see the doctor, an idea that I immediately rejected, as I thought there was nothing wrong with me. She and Dad had to drive me back to the town where I lived with Ellie, as I was still registered with their doctor's surgery. The doctor who I saw said that the mental health team would start seeing me when we returned to our local surgery. This sent my alarm bells ringing, as I had a vision of being forcefully taken away to a "mad house" in a straitjacket against my will. My knowledge of mental illness was poor at this time, as I had only seen films like *One Flew Over the Cuckoo's Nest* and formed a negative perception. I'm not proud of how I treated my family around this time. I even told Mum that she must have Alzheimer's and that she needed to be treated for mental illness, not me.

I should also mention that in July 2016, about a month before breaking up with Ellie, I had started taking medication for back pain that had been troubling me for several years. It was called amitriptyline, and it is also a drug used to treat depression. I started taking 10mg once per day for ten days, then increased to two per day. However, according to Ellie and my mum, I regularly didn't remember to take the tablets and apparently, I stopped taking them because I didn't like their side effects. The doctors we spoke to about my psychotic episode did not think this was part of the reason it happened in the first place, but we are not convinced about this. At the very least, we believe that stopping the medication didn't help the situation overall.

There are so many weird things I did around this time that I can't actually remember them very well, and in some cases I don't remember them at all. So, I sat down with my mum to chat about them. She remembers them better than anyone, as she was the unlucky person who had to deal with me.

## CONVERSATION WITH MUM

**James:** "So what are your main memories of this time, around August/September 2016?"

**Mum:** "Well, we obviously realised you were not well. It was the end of August, so it was quite nice weather. One morning you said to me that you wanted to go into London so that you could go into work and tell them you'd split up with your girlfriend. Then, you wanted to go for a walk, as it was a nice day, and find somewhere to help with your back problem."

**James:** "Was this after I had already been given the time off work?"

**Mum:** "No, it was before."

**James:** "So, it was a weekend?"

**Mum:** "No, it was a weekday, a day you should've been at work. I can remember standing by the front door and saying to you, 'Please James, please don't go, please don't do it.' You didn't go in the end, and I said that we needed to go to see the doctor, so we took you there."

**James:** "The one in Ware?"

**Mum:** "Yes. First, we went to Ware because that was where you were registered at the time. The doctor agreed that you obviously needed help, that you were delusional and said you needed referring to the mental health team. However, he couldn't do it because you were no longer living in his area.

So, we then had to take you to the GP in Abbots Langley, who referred you to the mental health team. There was a long wait for you to be seen, though – two weeks! I was really annoyed about that because I wanted you to be seen urgently. In the meantime, we just had to try and contain it at home."

**Mum:** "Then, there was the Sainsbury's incident where I had already taken Granny shopping in the morning before you, Dad and I went to a different supermarket to do our shopping. But you were convinced that I had already done our shopping when I went with Granny and that we were doing it all over again. You thought I had Alzheimer's at this point, and you told the Sainsbury's staff about this and that you were worried about me and Dad. This was embarrassing, as I had worked with one of them before when I was working at the Watford store!"

**James:** "Yeah, I remember that part and I still feel awful."

**Mum:** "It's okay, you were very ill. Anyway, that was that. There was also the train incident. You were on your way back from work. We used to pick you up from Watford Junction station. Dad was already on his way to Watford, but you phoned him and said you were getting off at Hemel Hempstead instead."

**James:** "I remember this incident as well, but I can't remember why I was going to Hemel. Maybe I missed the stop or something."

**Mum:** "Maybe. Dad then started driving to Hemel to meet you, but you contacted him again to say you had got off the train at Apsley, so he had to go to Apsley!"

**James:** "Poor Dad, I remember him shouting at me when I got in the car, and I had never seen him shout at me like that, especially since he had his stroke. I think I had made a mistake. I tried to see the funny side, but Dad just completely snapped at me, and I was genuinely quite scared. He had every right to react like this, of course."

**Mum:** "After this you got really fed up with us and said you were going out with your friend Chris and to meet a Tinder girl."

**James:** "Oh God, that's so cringe, on the same journey?"

**Mum:** "Haha, I'm not sure. But he said he was still at work when I phoned him. A few of your friends had got in touch with me and provided their phone numbers, as they had realised you were acting strangely and were concerned. So, when I phoned Chris, it became obvious you'd lied about going to see him. When you came back, you said you'd been trying to get a taxi and you couldn't get one. Rather than letting you go off with no specific place to go, I eventually agreed to your idea of spending a night at a hotel, as at least we would know where you were."

I remember the hotel incident. That night, I got so angry with my family that I decided I needed to spend a night away from them. I made poor Dad drive me to a local Premier Inn, where the lady at reception refused to give me a room, as she must have seen that there was something wrong with me. I went to the pub next door to the hotel and ordered a beer. Next thing I remember is two police officers asking me to come with them. They must have been informed that a man was behaving strangely and worrying staff and customers. I reluctantly got into their car, and they drove me back home and spoke to my parents. It wasn't long after this that another emergency service got involved – my family had to call me an ambulance when my behaviour became extremely concerning. Psychosis was in full force, and my world was about to completely fall apart.

# CHAPTER 4

# SECTIONED

My memories of this chapter of my life are blurred, to say the least. I think part of me wanted them to be erased because my behaviour was so far from who I really am, which is quite terrifying, really. I managed to find a print-out of my initial assessment from my first visit to A&E at Watford General Hospital. Below is what the hospital staff had to say:

## INITIAL ASSESSMENT

Date: 03/09/2016
Time started: 00:01

**Reason for referral / What do you want as an outcome from the referral?**

*Referred by out-of-hours GP. Family very worried, broke up with long-term girlfriend about two weeks ago and, since then, has been very emotionally upset. Not slept well for a few nights. Moved from home shared with girlfriend back to mother's address. Four days ago, started exhibiting pressured speech, incessant ramblings, disjointed conversation, often not making sense, paranoid that he and family were being spied on, believed that he was being headhunted by big companies.*

*Feels his mum is suffering from early-onset dementia. Very concerned that his younger brother Mark was messing about with his online accounts, and that many people were mistaking his identity for Mark and vice versa. Getting agitated when his family doesn't believe or understand these things, he reports. Was asked to take time off work this week, as employer found he wasn't making sense.*

*Was referred by GP to SPA (Single Point of Access) today. SPA gave an initial assessment appointment in two weeks' time. Family took him to out-of-hours GP surgery tonight at Watford hospital. GP referred to NIGHTCATT for assessment.*

**Mental health history** – *no history of mental health presentation before now*

**Family and personal history** – *no known family history of mental disorder*

*Mum, dad and auntie present at hospital tonight and appeared very concerned and supportive.*

*James now has belief that since he has been off sick for past few days, companies have been headhunting him, and he is in line for a promotion. He has no written or telephone communication to this effect, but somehow believes that this information is being relayed to him "through secure channels".*

*Had been with recent girlfriend for past three years, but they are now separated. Claims that girlfriend had some anxiety problems, which affected her drive and intimacy to the extent they were having relationship counselling. Girlfriend was throwing herself into work as a way of dealing with it. They shared a home together; since the break-up, James has moved back in with parents and brother.*

**Person's strengths and support networks:**
*Mum, dad, brother and auntie very supportive, also has very understanding friends.*

**Mental state examination:**

*We saw and assessed that his eye contact varied and fluctuated between fairly good eye contact with the interviewer, to constantly staring at his mum as he spoke. He was fairly calm, feeling tired. Speech was coherent but often illogical, especially when he tried to explain the nature of messages with regards to people confusing his and Mark's identity.*

*He felt his mood was good during the interview but acknowledged he had been tearful due to the break-up. Earlier in the evening, he became quite upset when trying to reason with Mark about not disclosing information on a YouTube video they had created. He even described Mark being taken away by the police and some civilians. (He claimed to have witnessed this, but his mum denies that Mark was ever taken.) In fact, James himself was brought home by police when staff at a local hotel found him to be "confused".*

*There were several ideas of reference from the TV and internet. He also thought the emergency bag in the GP's room was somehow connected to him and his family. He had a fixed belief that his mum was developing Alzheimer's and that his dad had serious memory problems, which was causing a lot of difficulty and, as such, he (James) needed to safeguard his family.*

*He described normal appetite and energy levels. Acknowledged poor sleep recently, and reported being up all night last night, as he was concerned Mark was about to do something with his online accounts and his smartphone.*

*He strongly denied any self-harming, suicidal or homicidal ideas or plans. He was orientated to time and place, but often seemed to think Mark was with us during the assessment, when he was clearly not. He claimed to be hearing and seeing Mark at the hospital.*

*There was a small window of insight as he acknowledged needing to recover and needing help, possibly medication to help him sleep and relax. He was happy to be seen and assessed* further by the service at his home, with effect from tomorrow. He was happy to try some sleep medication as of tonight. Mum and family had a preference to James receiving treatment and recovering at home, rather than in hospital. They assured us that they felt able to continue to support him, and work with the Crisis assessment and Home Treatment Team.

**Views of carer or other people involved in care and support:**
Mum (Caroline) is very much involved in James' care and has brought him in tonight for assessment. She is extremely frightened and concerned about what is happening to her son's mind and wants help urgently. She is happy to work with the service and facilitate home treatment, but felt the appointment offered by SPA for 15 September with the IA team was much too far away.

**Advice on driving** – advised not to drive as commencing sedating and new medication

**Assessor's overview and summary of mental health and social needs:**
- Symptomology of acute stress reaction/brief psychotic reaction
- Symptomology of first-episode psychosis
- No acute risk of harm to self; currently high risk of further deterioration in mental state and subsequent vulnerability if left untreated and without specialist support and monitoring
- No acute social needs

**Outline care plan:**
- Brief psycho-education counselling given tonight
- Treat sleep deprivation – zopiclone 3.75–7.5mg prescribed to commence tonight (4 × 3.75 tablets given)
- Family and James agreeable to commence further assessment and treatment at home with SWCATT as an alternative to hospital admission

- *James and family furnished with all CATT contact details and other helpful/useful contacts*
- *SWCATT to telephone at noon today and arrange home visit later (taking more zopiclone tablets if deemed appropriate)*
- *Family to contact NIGHTCATT immediately via telephone if any further acute deterioration tonight or contact emergency services if any endangerment*

As I mentioned in Chapter 3, I thought my brother had a motive against me. By the point the ambulance were called, I actually thought he might want to kill me.

I thought I was being watched at the time and I thought I was being tracked. I was puzzled who it was for a while, but at one point I came to the conclusion that Mark was behind it. He is always glued to his phone and tablet, and he's seen with his headphones on quite often, so my broken brain convinced me that he must have been tracking me on his devices. My paranoia that this was happening caused me to panic big time. I had the location setting on my phone permanently set to off. I even took off my Fitbit watch from my wrist because I didn't trust any form of technology.

It got even worse, though, because I somehow thought that some sort of explosive was going to go off at any point, which would end my life. *Was it planted in my phone or smartwatch?* This was going through my mind at the time, and I was really freaked out. I was also hearing a certain voice in my head that I wasn't convinced was my own. Because of this, I thought that an explosive could actually be inside me somewhere, and that it could be triggered by a certain word that I said.

The night that the ambulance was called was the first time in my time on earth that I genuinely thought I could die – apart from my childhood burger-choking incident, obviously. I had convinced myself that the voice inside my head was Mark and that he was going to end me. I became terrified of any loud noises because I thought I was under threat, and then the voice in my head became his. His voice sounded like a demon who was tormenting me. His voice convinced me that it was going to end. He even made me believe that he could kill me by killing himself, that because we were brothers, we were somehow in this together, and our lives were connected.

I remember being in my bedroom with my mum and dad. I was crying my eyes out and living in absolute terror of what could happen next. Then his voice in my head got louder, and he informed me he was at our front door with a gun to his head. I can't remember his exact words, but I remember him about to use the rude word that begins with C and rhymes with "hunt". Then I heard what sounded like a gunshot, and my parents turned around because it came from the front door. (It must've been a door knock.)

As one of them went to answer the door, I ran to my bed and jumped on it, hoping it would swallow me up like a black hole. I thought my evil brother was dead and that I was next. When the paramedics came into my room, I was scared to speak because I thought something I said would trigger my death. At this point I remember feeling faint and thinking my body was shutting down slowly. I remember thinking that there was nothing that I could do to stop my demise.

But somehow I had survived this mental torture and found myself, for the first time ever, in the back of an ambulance. I was very confused with what was happening and still scared to speak, so I tried to communicate with the people around me without actually putting sentences together. My French A-Level and beginner Spanish suddenly kicked in out of nowhere, and I was speaking sentences in a mixture of these languages as best I could. I thought that by doing this I would be safer, that the evil force wouldn't be able to detect what I was saying. The paramedics looked understandably baffled.

When we got to Watford General Hospital, I was taken to be assessed. However, my paranoia with loud noises was still there and got worse. Every time I heard a noise, such as a door closing, I thought it was dangerous, and it made me jump and panic. I still thought I was under threat and by this point, I thought other people who knew me were too. Because of my delusion that Mark could have killed himself, I wasn't sure what was out to get me anymore, but I was still convinced that something evil and terrible was happening.

After spending hours at the hospital, I was eventually sectioned under Section 2 of the Mental Health Act. My diagnosis was "acute psychosis with symptoms of schizophrenia". It was late at night, but I was taken in a taxi to a nearby psychiatric facility in Hertfordshire, where I would spend the next four weeks.

# CHAPTER 5

# LIFE INSIDE THE PSYCHIATRIC WARD

I can confirm that being sectioned is absolutely terrifying. I almost felt like I was going to prison, because I knew I would be spending four weeks in the same building without being allowed out.

When I arrived at the psychiatric ward, it was empty because all the other patients were in bed, as it was very late. This at least gave me a brief chance to familiarise myself with the new surroundings without any eyes on me. I remember the bloke working the night shift was very welcoming and kind to me, despite the fact I was still delusional.

After a successful night's sleep for a change, the next morning I was asked to start taking medication to get better, which I complied with, as I wanted to get out of there as soon as possible. I began to get to know some of my fellow patients, as well as learn the routine of the place. The food there was decent, and I remember eating quite a lot, as this was a side effect of the meds.

I spent the days getting to know everyone through group therapy sessions and general socialising. My favourite part of the experience was when the occupational therapist did an art session with us. Doing some simple drawings was a good distraction and an effective way to calm the mind.

We were allowed visitors at times, and my mum and dad came to see me as much as possible. The visits were very emotional. I would complain that I didn't want to be there and beg to be taken back home, which was very hard for my parents to deal with, as they were pretty much powerless to bring me home until I was well enough.

I eventually realised that the quickest way to get out was by complying with all that was asked of me. If I took my tablets and took part in the therapy, then that was the best I could do. I tried to get along with the other patients, despite some of them being quite difficult. I remember there were a few guys who I would play pool with, and I managed to persuade one of them to kick a football with me against a wall in the small garden area. I don't think he was that keen on this idea, and our kickabout didn't last long, but I was desperate to just be outside and not be so bored. I needed to occupy my mind. I wanted to do anything that would be a good distraction from how miserable and scary I was finding my situation.

Most of the time I got along fine with the other patients, but there were a few weird and unpleasant moments. One time, this older gentleman suddenly snapped at me out of nowhere and shouted right in my face, "F**k off, you c**t!" I could only come up with one potential reason as to why this happened: maybe I had invaded his personal space a little bit, and he didn't like anyone getting too close to him. Apart from that, I don't remember doing anything wrong, so I found it very surprising and obviously very rude of him. I didn't take it personally, though, as it occurred to me that he was very mentally ill too, maybe more than I was.

Another patient really freaked me out with his creepy actions. He had this habit of pacing up and down in parts of the ward, but he often gave me an odd and angry look as he was doing this. At some points, he also seemed to start coming towards me in an aggressive-looking way. I decided to avoid him at all costs and, if I had to get close, I made sure one of the staff members was near me, just in case he attacked me or anything.

At this point, my delusions had not gone away, and I came to a very odd conclusion that the creepy pacing guy was my brother's spirit in another person's body. I even shared this with Mum and Dad during one of their early visits, but Mum confirmed, "No, that is not him, he is at home in our house." I eventually believed this and stopped having delusions, due to getting more sleep and my medication taking effect.

The tablets I was taking also started to give me some major side effects, mainly making me very sleepy and sedated, and also giving me more of an appetite. I think the other patients were going through something similar too. We were fed the standard three meals a day, but this often wasn't enough. I remember a lot of us would regularly eat several slices of toast in the evenings after dinner and before bed – we were just constantly eating.

I had some much-needed comfort when Tommy made a phone call to the ward to speak to me. I don't have any memory of this conversation, but Tommy has since reminded me of something I said at the time, which I am not really proud of. Apparently, I said to him quite loudly down the phone, "Mate, everyone in here is f***ing nuts!" Normally I would keep thoughts like that to myself and not be so rude, but I was very unwell and not acting like myself. I guess the phone call must have happened quite soon after I joined the ward and was still getting used to the other patients. By the end of my stay there, I realised that, of course, the patients were not simply "nuts" but very ill, just like me. They were the same as all of us: just a bit broken and needing to get better.

I do have some small positive memories of the time I spent in the ward. I recall having good chats about all sorts of things with one guy who was a similar age to me. We would kick a ball about outside or watch one of the films that the place had available on DVD. This was nearer the end of my time there; I am pretty sure he was still there when I got out and was a bit gutted to see me go.

Finally, after what felt like the longest four weeks of my life, I was allowed to go home under the condition that people from the community mental health team would regularly check on me at my house. My time in the ward had not been the most pleasant experience, but it was necessary for me to be there to start my recovery. And yet, I had no idea of how difficult the next phase of getting better was going to be. It was a long road ahead with many challenges along the way.

# CHAPTER 6

# COMING BACK HOME

For the first time in a very long time, I was feeling a bit happier and more optimistic. I was sitting in the back of Mum's car on the way back home after four long weeks, so very relieved that I was out of the ward and going to be back living in the house I grew up in. It definitely felt like a step in the right direction.

But this didn't last very long. At first, I did enjoy having my freedom back; then, I got used to living at home again and realised that things were far from over. As part of the agreement with those who were looking after me, I had visitors almost every day in the form of social care workers. They needed to closely monitor my progress to make sure things were still slowly improving. Below is a letter from November 2016 that I dug out, a message to my GP from a psychiatrist in the mental health team looking after me.

## 9 NOVEMBER 2016

Dear Dr Jones,

**Primary mental health diagnosis:** *acute psychotic disorder with symptoms of schizophrenia*

**Care type:** *first episode psychosis (FEP)*

**Summary of appointment and current presentation:**

I reviewed Mr Lindsay in my outpatient clinic in Colne House on 4 November. He was accompanied by his mother, Caroline, and his care coordinator, Ioannis. I was pleased to hear that his mental health was more stable, but Mr Lindsay tells me that he is struggling somewhat with increased morning drowsiness.

He was initially detained under Section 2 of the Mental Health Act on 04/09/2016 at Kingfisher Court, when he presented with paranoia, ideas of reference, insomnia, wandering and over-valued ideas. Mr Lindsay is currently on the FEP pathway.

Mr Lindsay reports no issues with any of his family and tells me that they get on well.

Mr Lindsay has no difficulty with sleep initiation, and is frequently getting 9/10 hours of undisrupted sleep per night. He sets his alarm for 8am but does concede he has some difficulty waking. He tries to keep himself busy during the day. He goes shopping with his mother, attends gym classes and meets up with friends. He enjoys all of these activities, but does find that his drowsiness interferes with his ability to take full part in the gym classes. He enjoys reading books and watching programmes on Netflix. He is able to maintain his concentration throughout these activities.

He is very keen to get back to work as quickly as possible. He is currently awaiting an occupational health review organised by his employers.

On mental state examination, his speech was of normal volume and rate but somewhat monotone. His mood was subjectively low and objectively mildly depressed. This appears to be related to Mr Lindsay missing his ex-girlfriend, although they remain in contact as friends.

There are no anxiety or panic symptoms. He denies the presence of any auditory or visual hallucinations, and there is no evidence of any formal thought disorder.

*His movements have been slower than normal, and his appetite has increased, but he eats a balanced diet. His concentration has significantly improved since his discharge from hospital. There are no issues with his memory. He retains good insight into his mental health difficulties and is keen to continue on medication, as he feels as though it is beneficial and allows him to feel more like himself.*

### Care plan agreed with patient:

### Mental health medication:
Clonazepam 1mg BD and 2mg ON (reduced from 1mg TDS and 2mg ON)
Sodium valproate 800mg BD
Olanzapine 20mg ON

### Medication adherence support plans:
*Mr Lindsay is compliant with his medications*

### Side effects monitoring and physical health review:
*Mr Lindsay tells me that his appetite has increased, but there has been no noticeable weight gain.*

### Recovery goals and actions:
- *Continue to participate in activities and get out of the house*
- *Ensure compliance with medication*
- *Attend occupational health assessment*
- *Review with care coordinator next week to assess medication changes*
- *Care coordinator will kindly monitor mental state and response to medication reduction; Ioannis will be in contact with the medical team to discuss further plans*
- *Look out for any increased agitation or difficultly with sleep as signs of mental state instability*

The rest of 2016 ended up being quite rubbish, if I'm honest. I was still on heavy medication that gave me unpleasant side effects of feeling sleepy and generally very lethargic with little to zero energy. As Mum put it, I lost my "get up and go".

The aftermath of getting sectioned was very hard to take and difficult to face. Most of all I had an immense feeling of guilt and shame for the way I had behaved towards my family, particularly my brother, who I had accused of trying to harm me when I was unwell. I felt like I had destroyed the relationship we had as siblings, that I needed to rebuild it and make it up to him somehow. I was really sad by the idea that he used to look up to me, but thanks to this episode, I had destroyed our good relationship and betrayed him.

I was also reflecting a lot on my break-up. Part of me was questioning if I had done the right thing. I became quite regretful and kept asking myself why I didn't keep the relationship going longer and keep fighting for it. I wished I hadn't pulled the plug that resulted in my health breakdown. I fell into that trap of thinking what might have been: *could I have stayed healthy and avoided this fiasco?*

I was looking at my present and future in a very pessimistic way. I was now single and working a job I didn't like. I wasn't where I wanted to be – I was so far from it. It felt like I had hit rock bottom.

To be fair to my old employer, they handled the situation well. After a bit of time off when I returned home, they put together a phased return-to-work plan for me. They proposed that I worked two days a week to start, which were half days rather than full days. The prospect of going back to work was actually very appealing at the time because I was becoming increasingly bored at home.

I remember most days I would persuade Mum to go on walks with me – I wasn't the kind of person who could spend a lot of time indoors. During these walks, I would constantly complain about how annoyed I was of my situation, and how frustrated I was that I didn't do things differently. I would say things like, "I wish I could go back in time and save myself from the breakdown," and, "I have messed things up so much, my life is on the wrong track, and I can't fix it."

I would even go as far as saying things like, "I hate my life." As you can see, I got into some darker and depressed thoughts. Mum was my rock and would try her best to turn me back towards a glass-half-full way of thinking. She would remind me how lucky I was that I still had brilliant family and friends, and that things could be a lot worse, and I needed to focus on the positives. She was right, of course, but I found it hard to snap out of my state of mind. Things felt very bleak, and I was really struggling to see any sort of light at the end of the tunnel.

At this time, I don't think I was ever quite suicidal or anything, but this experience gave me an understanding of how people can get to that stage. When you've got nothing to look forward to, this can sometimes lead to more severe depression. I would go to bed at night dreading the next day ahead. Then I would stay in bed as late as lunchtime, thinking, "What is the point of getting up? There's nothing to get up for." I was lucky back then that I had things to keep me going – supportive family and friends, mainly, who never gave up on me, which made it possible to not give up on myself. Another thing that stopped me from being suicidal was imagining a world where I actually did give up my life. The thought of going through with something like that and upsetting family and friends was unbearable. Imagining a funeral scene where people were distraught and my parents were in tears, I could never let that happen and be the reason for so much pain and grief.

Nevertheless, I found it difficult to spend time with people because I would have nothing to offer in terms of what I was up to, and I didn't like talking about my life. I would also be jealous of things that other people had, like happy relationships and balanced states of mind without the help of medication. But despite all that, just spending time with different people would give me a little boost and keep me going.

When I eventually started going back to work, it initially felt very helpful. Even though I didn't like my old job much, I had at least some sense of purpose back. I was getting out of the house, spending time with different people and had some money coming in.

Earlier that year before my breakdown, I actually interviewed for a job at the same company but in a different department. It was essentially the same role, but doing different market research for different clients. In a nutshell, the data this team collected was for advertising purposes. I had always been keen on advertising since my uni days, so I went for this job, thinking that a fresh start within a new team with more interesting subject matter would be much more rewarding for me. I had a bit of rotten luck because I was verbally offered the role not long before having the breakdown. Fast-forward to when I finally returned to work after a few months, though, and they (understandably) had to offer the role to someone else. So, when I went back, I was frustratingly stuck in the same position.

Naively, I saw the phased return to work plan and thought, "Piece of cake, I got this." It seemed so simple that I would transition back into the swing of things.

The main obstacles to my success were the side effects of my medication. I found the process of commuting into London and trying to have productive days at work almost impossible. I ended up really cherishing my days off during the week. There were some days at work when I admitted to my manager that I was struggling so much, I had to go home early.

So, the year 2016 was coming to an end. Despite some highlights (pre-breakdown holidays to Edinburgh, Málaga and Devon, namely), it ended up being a pretty crap year, and I couldn't wait to see the end of it.

I thought that surely 2017 couldn't get any worse – could it?

# CHAPTER 7

# AFTERCARE AND GETTING MY LIFE BACK

The first half of 2017 just seemed like one big blur. All I remember was feeling miserable most days and weeks. I particularly hated work and my commute around this time.

I would get a lift from Mum or Dad to Watford Junction early in the morning. Then, I would get a train around 8am to London Euston. I guess most people on the train would read a book or listen to music or something, but I would take my seat and close my eyes for the entire journey (around 20 minutes). My medication had me so sedated, all I wanted to do was nap at every opportunity.

When we arrived at Euston, I dreaded the boring walk from that train to the Euston Square Underground Station. I was literally like a zombie walking down the street; I always felt down and exhausted. From there, I would take the Circle line (or Metropolitan line or Hammersmith & City line) to either Aldgate, Aldgate East or Tower Hill, whichever train came first. During my 15-or-so minutes on the Tube, I would − you guessed it − try and nap again. This part of the journey would be even worse if I didn't manage to get a seat. Then, the last part of the commute was walking from the Tube station to the office. When I first started working in London, I used to enjoy this bit, gazing up at the tall buildings and taking in all the scenery. But now, it was just 20 minutes of dreading the day ahead − a day of attempting to get work done and trying to overcome the side effects of my meds. So depressing.

Despite drinking copious amounts of tea and coffee during work hours, I spent most days at the office feeling exhausted and fed up. Fast-forward to the end of the working day, and I would be keen to get out of the office as soon as possible; I rarely stayed longer than I had to. The commute home was just the reverse of the morning – same rubbish mood, just a bit less of a need to nap. Then, getting back home would be followed by a few hours of dreading the next day I had to go to work and go through the whole ordeal again.

At work I had monthly meetings with HR and my manager to discuss the phased return and how I was feeling. I am grateful to my old employer for giving me time and trying their best to help me get back to full-time hours, but sadly it was never to be.

In hindsight, I wish I didn't accept things as they were back then, particularly with my medication. It took a long time to find the right meds for me, ones that would keep mental illness at bay, but also not sedate me at the same time.

I would advise anyone who has to get help for their mental health to **find the right formula.** If meds are not working for you, be honest with the doctor and seek out alternatives, which could be different meds or a form of therapy. **Don't accept things as they are if they are not working for you – there could be something better, and you deserve that.**

I should have requested alternative methods sooner. During my lunch breaks at work, I would sometimes go to a room that they had in the building used mostly as a prayer room. I figured out that no one used it in the middle of the day, so I would go in there and nap for half an hour. This isn't what someone should be doing every day on their lunch break, in my opinion. I was feeling so sedated, it was ridiculous.

At this point in my life, I also wasn't looking after my physical health in the same way that I do today. Namely, I wasn't doing any exercise and I wasn't eating well. The only exercise I had was the slow, miserable walking as part of my commute, and occasionally on weekends I would go on walks with Mum and have a moan.

I know now **how important staying active and eating well are for mental health.** Back then, my tablets left me with zero motivation to exercise and with no self-esteem, either, which made me reluctant to socialise with friends.

Another thing getting me down was that I couldn't get over the break-up from the year prior. I wanted to get back together with Ellie. I wrongly thought if that happened, then I would start to become happy again.

We actually did meet up on a few occasions to do things like go to the cinema, and at one point, I told her that I wanted her back. She said she would think about it, but the next time we met up, she admitted that it wouldn't be a good idea because we would just get into the same problems that made us break up last time.

She was right — of course she was. This was hard for me to take, but I needed to hear it. I tried to suggest that we could continue to hang out at friends, but she said that wasn't a good idea either. I remember one of her WhatsApp messages as clear as day. It said, "You will always be a special part of my life, but I think it is time for both of us to move on."

Even though this upset me — crushed me, even — it was definitely the closure that both of us needed. It took me a while to get over this, but eventually I realised we did the right thing.

Meanwhile, my attempts to get back to full-time work were proving unsuccessful. It wasn't just the meds that were preventing this — I'd just had enough of working in the industry. The job didn't suit me and was going nowhere.

It was during one of my monthly HR-and-manager meetings that they broke the news to me. I was quite surprised it happened at the time; I naively wasn't expecting it. HR explained to me that, if it wasn't for my mental illness situation, there was a possibility that they would have to go down the disciplinary route with me anyway. This was due not only to my lack of full-time hours, but because my general performance on the job was not at an expected standard.

I was told that I would be leaving the company in the form of a settlement agreement. It was all quite complicated, but essentially, I was sort of being made redundant.

This happened at the start of summer 2017, and I remember being quite relieved and pleased with the decision overall. I was being given some money and I would no longer have to do my dreaded commute and job anymore. I did want to get out of the situation on my own terms and would have preferred to do it that way. But to be honest, maybe this was exactly what I needed at the time. Maybe it was a blessing in disguise?

# CHAPTER 8

# NEW MEDICATION AND UNEMPLOYMENT

The second half of 2017 was quite different from the first. I was now unemployed and registered for Job Seeker's Allowance. I initially enjoyed the first month of this, treating it as a bit of a break. There was no point in rushing back to get another job, so I gave myself about month for the dust to settle.

When it came to finding another role, I was somewhat torn about how to approach this. I had about four years of market research experience, so I could have tried to get back into that. But there didn't seem much point in doing that, as I would almost definitely not enjoy being back in that world again.

The alternative was to get a different type of job. I had a master's degree in marketing, and I desperately wanted to start using it. The only thing that didn't appeal to me was starting again at the bottom of the career ladder, so to speak. I spoke to many people for advice and realised that I should try and pursue the marketing career. What is the point of spending a great deal of your life working if you're not doing something you are passionate about? I decided that I needed to **put fulfilment first.**

During the summer, I also made a step in the right direction in terms of medication. After complaining to the doctor that I was suffering too much from side effects, they decided to put me on a different drug: an anti-psychotic called aripiprazole.

This proved to be a good move. There were still some side effects of this stuff – I still felt sedated to an extent, but nowhere near as badly as I did on the previous meds.

I also made a bold decision to enter a local 10k run. This was a run that I had done many years before in Abbots Langley called the "Tough Ten". I was in no shape to do it at the time, but I saw it as motivation to finally get fit and lose some of the weight that I had gained since having my breakdown and being on meds. I signed up to the run around June and it was in September, so I had time to get fitter.

I joined a gym around this time too, not only to exercise but also to have something to actually do with my time and get out of the house. I don't think the gym membership lasted long, though. I remember running on a treadmill to try and get fit for the 10k, but realised I found the treadmill so boring! No offense, treadmill fans, but it wasn't for me.

I started going for runs outside instead – sometimes I even attempted to do some of the route that the 10k would be covering. Sadly, most of the time, I couldn't actually run that far due to the medication holding me back. Bloody meds! I would call Mum to come and pick me up in her car, and this became quite a regular occurrence.

I wish I had realised back then that the aripiprazole was still not quite the right solution for me. I should have raised this with the doctor and tried to get myself on a more suitable drug. But back then I thought that these meds were as good as it was going to get. I became particularly frustrated that doctors would advise me to use exercise as a way to improve my mental health (which is the right advice), but how was I supposed to exercise when the meds were holding me back? It's a really difficult situation for anyone. I felt like I was running along with huge weights attached to my body.

Anyway, I kept trying to prepare for the 10k, but when the day eventually came, I knew I still wasn't going to do well. I did the race with Chris, my good friend from school, and thankfully for me he had not trained much either – at least we could struggle together! On the next page is a pic of us at the start of the run.

That was probably the toughest 10k I have ever done; I had to stop and walk several times. I really had to push myself more than ever, not only because I really wanted to beat Chris – I can get pretty competitive – but I didn't want to finish last out of the hundreds of participants. Looking back, I am just proud of finishing the race. I think anyone who takes aripiprazole will agree with me that certain medications and running simply do not mix, so finishing the run felt like a minor miracle! Below is a pic from the end of the race, and you can tell the difference between this one and the pre-race shot!

In October 2017, I had another check-up with the mental health team. Here is the brief letter that they sent to my GP:

## 26 OCTOBER 2017

**Primary mental health diagnosis:** acute polymorphic psychotic disorder with symptoms of schizophrenia

**Summary of appointment and current presentation:**
*Mr Lindsay attended his outpatient appointment with me on 13 October 2017, together with his mother and a senior associate practitioner.*

*We recently changed his medication from olanzapine to aripiprazole due to on-going side effects of sedation. He feels he is doing better on aripiprazole and he feels less subdued, more active and no longer oversleeps.*

*There are no signs of relapse.*

**Mental health medication:**
Aripiprazole 20mg OD

**Risk review:** *As he has changed medication, there is a risk of relapse.*

**Recovery goals and actions:**
- *Advised to continue current medications*
- *Would recommend going back to work*
- *Healthy diet and daily exercise recommended*

About a month after the 10k run, I was lucky enough that Mum and Dad decided to take us on a holiday to Lanzarote in the Canary Islands. It was a nice break for me in terms of getting away from the dull routine I was stuck in – applying for jobs, going for the occasional interview, getting rejection after rejection.

Normally I would have enjoyed this type of holiday a lot more, but thanks to aripiprazole, it was not as good as it could have been. Instead of swimming in the pool and taking part in all the hotel activities, such as archery, tennis and football, all I wanted to do was nap in the shade on a sunbed all day. I couldn't really have many cold beers or cocktails either, as that would just make the sedating effect of medication even worse.

When we got back from that holiday in November, I was getting really fed up of the meds and how they were making life so much harder. When New Year's Eve finally came around, I decided that 2018 was going to be better – it surely could not get much worse than the last year and a half.

I ended up taking quite a drastic decision, one than I am not proud of and something I know that I should have done differently. At some point at the end of 2017/start of 2018, I decided to stop taking medication completely. **Please be advised that this is most certainly not the right way to come off meds – don't do it.**

To make things worse, I hardly told anyone about what I had started doing. I began a new daily process of opening up the tablet, then flushing it down the toilet instead of taking it. As far as most people were concerned, including family, I was still taking the tablets.

This had a drastic effect on my daily life going forward. At first it seemed like I might have done the right thing, but eventually, this decision backfired in a big way.

# MENTAL HEALTH APPS

I want to step away from the main story briefly - as I have already done and will continue to do throughout the book - to share the apps I have discovered which help me with mental well-being. I should point out that I am also mindful of spending too much time on phones or looking at screens, but I think these apps are somewhat of an exception due to their benefits. There are thousands of apps out there to choose from, but these are ones that have worked for me:

- **Headspace** (iPhone or Android): I have signed up to the premium version of this because I think it's the best meditation app available. There's a huge variety of meditations to try, and once you get the hang of the basics, you can do things like mindful walking, listening to focus music, getting help sleeping and much more.
- **Calm** (iPhone or Android): I have tried the premium level of this as well, and, in my opinion, it's not as good as Headspace, but it's a great cheaper alternative, as it has a lot of the same features. I personally don't love the voices of the presenters, but everyone has their preferences, and you might love them.
- **WorryTree** (iPhone or Android): Record, manage and problem-solve your worries and anxiety based on cognitive behavioural therapy (CBT) techniques. I found this useful for figuring out if a worry is something I can deal with or one I have no control over.
- **Strava** (iPhone or Android): This technically isn't a mental health app, but I find it is the perfect app for exercise due to the social features. I will go on this daily, purely because I like seeing what friends and family are up to and giving them "kudos" for their activities. It's also great to

record your workouts because I find it is more impactful seeing all those numbers, such as distance and calories burned.

- **Finch: Self Care Widget Pet** (iPhone): This is a handy little self-care app that will make you feel more prepared for things in your life, and it also encourages positivity. The idea is you get given a "self-care best friend" or pet to take care of, and taking care of it helps you learn to look after yourself!
- **Depression CBT Self-Help Guide** (Android): This one is worth getting if you have or think you have depression. It contains a great deal of mental health information, so it provides plenty of good education on depression, as well as the best strategies for managing the symptoms.

# CHAPTER 9

# EMPLOYMENT FINALLY LEADS TO A NEW LEASE ON LIFE

In January 2018, I finally got myself a job – well, sort of.

I had the idea of approaching one of my old employers for quite a few months, but I saw it as a last resort because there were several reasons I didn't want to go back there. I didn't leave on the best terms with my line manager. Also, the work itself was not what I wanted to do, nor was the industry where I wanted to be.

I knew that this company was always looking for temps to do some basic data-entry work on zero-hour contracts. It was how I originally got into the company on a full-time basis back in the day (around 2013).

I was putting off contacting them for a long time, but I ended up getting so desperate for any sort of job as something to do. So, I emailed the data services manager in the end, and he offered me some part-time work, just like that. I was actually happy at the time because I finally had something to give me more of a sense of purpose, something to get me out of bed in the morning. I also got a little bit of disposable income, and I really needed that after so many months without it.

I started working there, and it felt really awkward at first, seeing so many old colleagues who I thought I wouldn't see again. My old manager was from the client services team, not data services where I was temping. To be fair to him, he came up to me on the first day back, we shook hands, and he asked how I was doing in a genuine, friendly way. There was no bad blood in the end, and being back working there was not as bad as I thought it would be, in terms of the people and environment.

The job itself was boring as hell, but at least it was a no-pressure, take-it-easy type of gig. In some ways, that was what I needed to ease back into working again.

I also started volunteering the month after. I was a part-time volunteer marketing assistant at a charity based in Hatfield called Groundwork East. At first, I was not sure about volunteering, but I am so glad I did it, and it ended up being a very worthwhile decision. I was grateful to Mum, who persuaded me to go for it.

Away from work, I was enjoying spending time with friends and being off meds. I was able to be myself again, and I could have a few beers if I wanted without the concern that alcohol would make the medication side effects worse.

Around springtime of this year, some of the boys from uni and I decided to plan a week in Porto, Portugal. This was the first time I had properly enjoyed a holiday since becoming unwell. We stayed in an Airbnb, and it was non-stop fun and laughter from start to finish, made even better by beautiful warm weather. We went to the beach and did some body-boarding, we walked around the city and sampled the local ice cream, we visited a port distillery, and of course we had many nights out at the bars and pubs, including a very nice rooftop bar.

Things were finally starting to look up. I was feeling so much better because I wasn't on any meds. I had loads more energy, and my mind felt very clear, the clearest it had felt in a very long time. I was not fond of my data entry job, but when I was doing my other volunteering job, I was loving it. I was finally doing a type of role that I had studied for at uni.

The charity was fantastic, and I had a brilliant manager who gave me the chance to work on all sorts of things, including social media, events, blogs and press releases – proper interesting and fulfilling stuff. I very much had a new lease on life and was starting to feel more positive and optimistic about my present and future.

I was fully committed to pursuing a career in marketing, preferably in the charity sector. This sector was a breath of fresh air compared to my previous corporate roles. All my colleagues were so passionate and a joy to work with. I really fell in love with Groundwork as a charity. They run all sorts of environmental community projects, such as garden clearance services for elderly and vulnerable people, and outdoor education sessions for children and their families. They do incredible work, and I felt genuinely proud to represent them.

I kept working the two jobs for a while. I think it was around June or July that Groundwork offered to start paying me on a part-time, zero-hour contract. I was pretty delighted by this, because it meant that I could afford to quit the other job that I didn't like. Now, my week was taken up by two paid days at Groundwork, plus however many hours they could offer me on a voluntary basis. Most weeks I did two days paid, and one or two days volunteering, giving me some spare time with the rest of my week.

I had also managed to stay stable in terms of my mental health, although I was still living a bit of a lie, with most people thinking I was still on meds. I did admit to a couple of friends that I was off my medication – I couldn't bear to keep it all to myself. They were both understanding of my reasons and accepted the fact that I seemed to be doing a lot better at that moment.

The year 2018 was somewhat significant in terms of my fitness as well. Thanks to a lack of meds holding me back, I had a great deal of energy and motivation. This led to me doing all sorts of things with my spare time; my health and fitness went from strength to strength – pardon the pun.

# MUSIC AND MENTAL HEALTH – MY PLAYLIST FOR YOU

It's fair to say that music has the power to put us in a good mood, and the right music can also get us through the hardest of times.

Below are some songs that I have found to be particularly useful. I hope they can help you in some way too. They might help you keep going during a walk or run, they might help you have a cry, they might cheer you up... no matter what, listen and enjoy!

- "Bad Life" by Sigrid and Bring Me the Horizon
- "Anxiety" by Julia Michaels featuring Selena Gomez
- "Pennyroyal Tea" by Nirvana
- "Misguided Ghosts" by Paramore
- "Secret for the Mad" by dodie
- "One More Light" by Linkin Park
- "Head Above Water" by Avril Lavigne
- "Who You Are" by Jessie J
- "No Bad Days" by Bastille
- "F**kin' Perfect" by P!nk
- "Hate That You Know Me" by Bleachers
- "Mountain At My Gates" by Foals
- "Pretty Shining People" by George Ezra
- "Hold On" by Wildwood Kin
- "Harmony Hall" by Vampire Weekend
- "Now I'm in It" by HAIM
- "How to Save a Life" by The Fray
- "Little Talks" by Of Monsters and Men
- "Lose You to Love Me" by Selena Gomez

- "I Don't Think I'm Okay" by Bazzi
- "Fleabag" by YUNGBLUD
- "Keep Your Head Up" by Ben Howard
- "KEEP IT UP" by Rex Orange County
- "This Is Me" by Keala Settle and *The Greatest Showman* Ensemble
- "Hunger" by Florence + The Machine
- "Help!" by The Beatles
- "Breathe Me" by Sia
- "Rose-Colored Boy" by Paramore
- "Good Grief" by Bastille
- "Skyscraper" by Demi Lovato
- "breathin" by Ariana Grande
- "Vienna" by Billy Joel
- "People, I've been sad" by Christine and the Queens
- "Surface Pressure" by Jessica Darrow
- "In My Blood" by Shawn Mendes
- "Perfect" by Anne-Marie
- "Best Fake Smile" by James Bay
- "Free" by Florence + The Machine

# CHAPTER 10

# SPORT AND EXERCISE TO THE RESCUE

So, I got involved in so many things during this year, it's hard to keep track and remember what I did and when! I think it all started when I began to attend an indoor circuit-training class, which was literally about a ten-minute walk from where I was living. I discovered that these types of classes were a million times better than going to a gym on your own (which I had tried and failed prior to this), not to mention cheaper! I personally think group exercise is the way forward. You motivate each other, laugh together, struggle together, and then feel sore together the next day. When I first went to this class, I was quite unfit, but gradually, week by week, I started feeling better and better. This, combined with eating well, meant I was able to slowly lose the weight I had gained the previous year.

Since I had a bit more spare time due to not quite working full-time hours, I had more opportunities to partake in activities that I enjoyed. One of these was joining a local tennis club, doing a sport I have always enjoyed. The group tennis lessons were just as beneficial as the circuit class – a combination of having fun and getting a good workout.

The next activity I discovered is still a huge passion of mine to this day. I decided to get up early one Saturday morning and try my local parkrun, which takes place in Watford's Cassiobury Park. It was a beautiful, sunny spring morning, I was surrounded by keen runners and glorious nature, and I loved every second of it. I had been doing running wrong all this time – running alone or on a treadmill is nothing compared to a parkrun. This became something I would do almost every Saturday morning. I also took advantage of how many great local parkruns there are in my area, such as St Albans and Hemel Hempstead.

So I was slowly becoming a more and more active person. I realised how exercise has brilliant benefits for mental well-being. It makes you feel happier and does wonders for self-esteem and confidence.

I was also starting to go on more dates as I started experiencing these benefits. I took advantage of the apps available, including Hinge, Bumble and Tinder. I was well and truly over my ex by this point and had really started to feel good about myself at last. None of the dates led to anything particularly serious, but I was okay with that. I felt like I was really starting to get my life back.

I wasn't done with discovering more feel-good sport and exercise. I found out that there was a special kind of football session being held near where I lived. This was (and still is) ran by the charity Watford FC Community Sport and Education Trust. The project goes by the name of "Man On!", and it is aimed at men aged 18 and over who are looking for support with their mental well-being. It's designed to support men with their mental health through physical activity and a conversation café.

I was completely sold after the first session! I had always enjoyed playing football, but this session was different. There was some competitiveness, but no pressure whatsoever, and it was so laid back and friendly. It wasn't like some five-a-side experiences I have had before, where you encounter aggressive men with rubbish attitudes who get annoyed at you if you don't play well. Man On! was a breath of fresh air, and I had never had such a good time playing football. The conversation café part was fantastic as well. It was half an hour of safely discussing mental health as a group, with useful tips and advice shared in a comfortable environment (and free tea and biscuits too – win). This became one of the highlights of my week almost every week, but I still didn't stop there!

Up until this point, I had been driving to work. My house to the office was about a 20-minute drive without traffic, but it could take up to 45 minutes with traffic. One day I decided to look on Google Maps to find out how long it would take me to cycle there – that's right, cycle! It estimated that the ride would be a whopping 1 hour and 15 minutes. At first, I thought, "No thanks, too much, no chance I am doing that!" But then one morning, I thought, "Sod it, why not!?"

The journey turned out to be a truly epic adventure of an experience. It was exhausting, don't get me wrong, but the difference in my mood at work during the day was massive. I loved being able to cycle past all of the cars sitting in traffic. It was a mostly flat route too, and half of the route involved an amazing cycle path that I fell in love with. It's called Alban Way, and it goes from St Albans to Hatfield. If you are local to the area, I would definitely encourage trying it. It used to be an old railway line, and it is a very pretty and peaceful route to cycle. With that, I became one of those people who love their commute! It was absolute heaven compared to my old slog of a commute to London the year before.

I was also filling a lot of my spare time with trips to the cinema this year (on my own this time). It was something I had started doing in 2017, and it became a regular hobby. The problem was that it gets expensive if you are going to the pictures every week and paying nearly a tenner each time. I discovered a great solution to this problem, and I think to this day it is one of the best decisions I have made in recent years. I finally took the plunge and decided to join Cineworld Unlimited, where you pay the same price every month to have as many cinema visits as you want.

I have enjoyed going to the movies my entire life, but this year it became a real passion of mine, and I realised its therapeutic benefits. In this day and age where we spend too much time on our smartphones, a great thing to do is turn your phone off for two hours and immerse yourself in a great film. My closest Cineworld at the time was in Hemel Hempstead, a 15-minute drive or 30-minute cycle from where I was living. I remember very fondly spending afternoons cycling to the cinema, watching a movie with a tasty coffee and snacks, cycling home and feeling brilliant from the three or four hours well spent.

The cinema became like a second home or a church to me. I would go there and completely relax, de-stress and escape. I didn't care that most of my visits were alone. This was some excellent me-time − some of the best me-times ever. Some of my friends would even joke, "Do you live at the cinema?!"

Around this time, I also took another significant step forward in terms of my recovery. Up until that point, I had been quite closed up when it came to the subject of my mental illness. I didn't really like to talk about it, and I viewed it and something I wanted to forget about completely. I never really discussed it openly with anyone, as I wasn't keen on the idea. But this slowly started to change. Rather than bury it, I slowly decided to learn more about it, and eventually start sharing what I knew and experienced.

# MENTAL HEALTH MOVIES AND PROGRAMMES

Over the years there have been many good portrayals of mental health in both film and television. I think these are so important to help everyone understand it better, as well as normalising it and ending stigma. These are my recommendations that I have seen – check them out if you can. I find that, as a mental illness sufferer, watching things like these makes me more comfortable with my own condition, and able to open up and discuss it with others.

- *My Mad Fat Diary* (series)
- *David Harewood: Psychosis and Me* (documentary)
- *Silver Linings Playbook* (film)
- *13 Reasons Why* (series)
- *Stacey Dooley: On the Psych Ward* (documentary)
- *It's Kind of a Funny Story* (film)
- *Inside Out* (film)
- *One Flew Over the Cuckoo's Nest* (film)
- *Still Alice* (film)
- *Losing It: Our Mental Health Emergency* (series)
- *The Mind, Explained* (series)
- *Homeland* (series)
- *Beautiful Boy* (film)
- *Side Effects* (film)
- *Girl, Interrupted* (film)
- *Joker* (film)
- *Joe Wicks: Facing My Childhood* (documentary)
- *The Fisher King* (film)

- *The Hours* (film)
- *Little Miss Sunshine* (film)
- *The Perks of Being a Wallflower* (film)

# CHAPTER 11

# MENTAL HEALTH MEDIA WORK

Once again, I have Mum to thank. She talked to me during a car journey one day about my condition and coming to terms with it. At first, I did not want to bring all my negative thoughts and experiences of psychosis flooding back. I had moved on and I wanted to keep the experience shut away, buried deep. Mum revealed that she had read a good book about someone who had been sectioned several times, and she recommended it.

The book was about none other than former boxing heavyweight world champion, Frank Bruno. I had heard of him, but I was not someone who followed boxing very much. I had no idea that this person had been through some very traumatic experiences after his retirement from boxing. I decided to give his book a read, and then I could not stop reading it or put it down.

I could not believe how much I related to this book. There were plenty of parallels between what he had gone through and my experience. It really changed my perspective. I was in awe of Frank because he didn't hold back in telling his story. His book, called *Let Me Be Frank*, is a very powerful and emotional read that I would thoroughly recommend to everyone.

That book had huge significance for me personally because I finally realised the power of sharing a story like that. Reading someone else describe a situation similar to mine gave me enormous comfort. Not only that, but I was inspired to start sharing my own story for the very first time.

That's the beauty of reading books – they let you discover a story in your own time and at your own pace and comfort. I went on to read many other incredible books on mental health later on in life, including titles by Matt Haig, Bryony Gordon and Bella Mackie, to name a few.

It was thanks to Frank's incredible bravery that I slowly became braver and braver. One evening I was browsing the website of Mind, the mental health charity. I saw that part of their site was dedicated to guest blog posts from people who have suffered with mental illness. Then, I had one of those light-bulb moments – I could submit a blog post to them myself.

After discussing this with Mum, I decided it was well worth doing. She rightly pointed out the potential benefits and drawbacks of doing this. I had to be aware that I was exposing myself to online discrimination, and if it got published, it was out there for anyone to see. Despite this, I still wanted to go through with it. My experience with psychosis is easily the worst thing I have ever gone through – I wouldn't wish it on my worst enemy. So, if I could help just one person by sharing my story, it was worth doing. Anyone who has experienced something this traumatic needs to know that it gets better. I loved the idea of giving other people hope.

I sat at my laptop one evening, and all the words kind of fell out of me onto a Word document. I managed to describe my experience in about one page or so. I could not believe how therapeutic it was to write about this stuff – I had discovered a healthy outlet.

I was delighted when the person at Mind confirmed that they would publish it on their website. My emotions were all over the place when it came out; I was a mixture of excited and very nervous. You can find the article through the list of links at the end of the book.

I then had another little brainwave: I could post the link to the blog on my social media channels. I discussed with Mum again, just for peace of mind. I now finally felt ready to "come out" to everyone about this experience. It was a huge moment for me personally. I was no longer feeling ashamed of what happened – I was owning it and accepting that it was a part of who I was.

I will never forget the aftermath of sharing it on socials. I was so overwhelmed with how it was received. I think out of all the things I had shared on Facebook (including graduation photos and my ski season), this blog post had the biggest reaction in terms of likes and comments.

I was afraid of how people would react, but the feedback was extremely positive. The notifications flooding my feed said things like, "You are so brave," and "This is so inspiring." I felt so very happy and relieved.

The story also led to lots of people messaging me about their own mental health experiences, both friends who I knew and strangers who I had never met. I was pleasantly surprised at how honest and open people were, and I learnt things about people that I was very grateful to them for sharing with me. Things like how they had been taking medication for anxiety or depression, or how they had been going to counselling or therapy, or how they had to deal with grief after losing someone close, or asking me for advice for either themselves or another person struggling... all sorts of things.

I made sure I replied to everyone. I didn't have all the answers, of course, but I appreciated being contacted and having the chance to help people where I could.

This wonderful experience was another very positive step forward in terms of my recovery and personal journey. I was now in a good place and really enjoying life. Writing and sharing the blog did wonders for me, and it also gave me determination to do even more. I had realised by this point that there was a lot of stigma and misunderstanding around mental illness. I wanted to do everything in my power to help people and inspire others, and I had caught the writing bug.

# CHAPTER 12

# TIME TO COME CLEAN

The summer of 2018 was definitely one to remember fondly. One of my best friends from uni was getting married in August. At the beginning of this month, we had his stag party in Birmingham (where he is from originally). I stayed in a hotel for the weekend with two of the guys.

By this point I was very into my parkruns. I had discovered that there was a parkrun quite near to where we were staying. So, after the first night at the hotel and before the afternoon of the stag, my friend Dan and I got up early on the Saturday morning and did the Canons Park version of the parkrun. It was after the run that Dan came up with a fantastic idea.

He said to me, "If you want to do more to help people with mental illness, why don't we do the Great South Run in Portsmouth in October, and we can fundraise for Mind!"

I was super keen on this – "Let's do it!" The Great South Run is ten miles, so it gave us a few months to train.

After that conversation, the stag party itself was so much fun. Thanks to being off meds and the great year I was having so far, I was really able to enjoy my social life to its full potential. We were all dressed up as *Peaky Blinders* characters and got really drunk. To this day, I think we all agree it was one of the best stags we have had so far.

The wedding weekend later that month was also incredibly good. Once again, I was able to find a parkrun near to our hotel the morning before the wedding started. This time it was the Lowestoft parkrun with my friend Jack. It was a beautiful run by the coast, and I managed to get a new PB (personal best). I was getting fitter and faster!

The reception part of the wedding was amazing – another hilarious drunken party with the uni gang, one never to be forgotten.

I had plenty more to look forward to that summer. A couple of months before, I had decided to treat myself and book a holiday. I ended up discovering these so-called "activity holidays", where you spend a week doing water sports, cycling, tennis and things like that. I booked a week in Turkey for the beginning of September. This seemed right up my street, considering all the sport and exercise stuff I had been enjoying recently.

Then, not long after I booked that, another opportunity presented itself out of nowhere. I was hiking with my uni friends Jack and Tom around mid-August. Jack was telling us about his friend from school who had recently broken up with his girlfriend. Turns out they had a holiday in Sri Lanka booked together, so Jack was taking her place instead. He casually said to us, "Yeah, it should be a great adventure. You two should come along if you like?"

Tom and I were like, "Er, YES PLEASE." We booked the time off work straight away. The two weeks in Sri Lanka were at the end of September. My manager at work admitted it wasn't ideal for me to be off, but I was taking advantage of being on a zero-hour contract: I could essentially have time off whenever I wanted, unlike being on a permanent contact.

So, August was really good – now I had two holidays in September to look forward to, and I was loving life!

However, I was feeling more and more guilty about the lie I was living. I was still not taking medication and throwing tablets down the toilet every day. I wanted to start telling people but I was terrified. I had this fear in my mind that if I admitted what I had been doing since the start of that year, it would lead to me being sectioned again. Eventually, I decided to phone the Mind Infoline. This was a confidential service through which you could speak to one of their volunteers over the phone. I told this lady everything, and she assured me that I would not be sectioned or anything, and maybe I should think about telling my GP before telling my family. This made me feel significantly better.

I went and saw my local GP next, and the doctor was very understanding with me about the whole thing. She admitted that I did the wrong thing by coming off tablets out of the blue and not gradually, which I already knew was a stupid decision. Again, I felt loads better getting all this off of my chest. Now I just needed to tell Mum, which still scared me.

I sat down with her in our lounge and came clean. Her reaction was not too bad, but she made it clear she was disappointed in me, and I think the whole thing hurt her, which was completely understandable. It was a selfish and reckless decision by me, but she did admit that she understood why I decided to do it, since she knew how much I was not getting on with medication.

I was so relieved that the truth was finally out. One of the things that pushed me to admit my wrongdoing was the blog. I wanted to do more blog writing and I realised that I could not be a fraud. If I was going to write about this stuff, people deserved to know only the truth about my experiences.

Mum and I eventually got back to normal. In fact, she was proud that I had managed to come off meds (despite doing it the wrong way). We agreed that I was going to be straight with her from now on.

I felt great now that I could move on without the guilt, and I was looking forward to the travels I had coming up. I also had more writing in the pipeline for Trigger Publishing. They are a company devoted to improving mental wellness through books, advice, content and resources.

Not only this, but I had been in touch with my old universities (Portsmouth and Hertfordshire) regarding how I could share my experience through their channels. This led to my participation in an event being organised for October of that year. I was going to do a presentation at the University of Hertfordshire all about my mental illness and things that have helped me during my recovery. My training for the Great South Run was going well too, and the next few months were full of potential!

# THINGS YOU SHOULDN'T SAY TO SOMEONE EXPERIENCING MENTAL ILLNESS

Since becoming unwell myself and going through recovery, I am definitely more mindful of stigma and certain things that I hate hearing. Some things apply to men only, but I think it's always important to show empathy and be considerate of how words that you say could be interpreted. Someone could be going through depression or anxiety, or just generally having a rubbish time, and what you say could add to their hardship.

Thankfully, we are now living in a much more accepting and inclusive society, but be sure to be careful before you tell anyone you come across…

- "Man up."
- "Snap out of it."
- "Grow a pair."
- "Get over it."
- "Stop being so paranoid."
- "You're mad/mental/crazy."
- "Cheer up."
- "You're a psycho."
- "Everyone is like that, though."
- "Pull yourself together."
- "Stop being so negative all the time."
- "Be a man."
- "I'm a bit OCD."
- "Committed suicide" – the correct phrasing is "died by suicide".

# CHAPTER 13

# TRYING NEW THINGS IN NEW COUNTRIES

The Turkey trip was the first time I had been outside of the UK on my own for a holiday. My ski season was the only exception to this; that was for six months, and Turkey was for one week.

I would highly recommend visiting different parts of the world to anyone. Specifically for those who have experienced mental illness, I think it really helps in several ways. It gives you a great sense of perspective and makes you feel very accomplished. It also allows you to "escape" from the ups and downs of everyday life, it can provide new ideas and more motivation, and it gives you more confidence and independence.

Sometimes going to another country presents the opportunity to try new things as well, which I decided to grab with both hands. I managed to have a bunch of new, exciting experiences on this holiday, some of them were even a bit outside of my comfort zone! These included:

- **Scuba diving:** I only went five metres under the sea, but that was enough for my liking! It was beautiful down there, though, and it made me wish I could permanently breathe underwater (a superpower I have wanted since childhood).
- **Water skiing:** This is much harder than it looks. I fell off so many times and ingested a lot of sea water.
- **Wakeboarding:** This is quite similar to water skiing, but it involved surprisingly less falling off in my case.

- **Paddleboarding:** I would highly recommend trying this. In my group we all attempted doing headstands on the board, which was hilarious, particularly when I fell off and into the water (sensing a pattern here).
- **Windsurfing:** This was another harder-than-it-looks thing for me, but so much fun once you get the hang of it – and yes, I fell off a lot.

In addition to all those wonderful water sports, there were plenty of things to enjoy on land that I was more familiar with: tennis, mountain biking, running, yoga classes, sunbathing, eating lots of yummy food, going on boozy boat trips and visiting lovely local restaurants. I had a blast. I met a bunch of nice new people as well, which I think is always one of the best things about visiting new countries and places.

I think the whole experience did wonders for my confidence, which had taken a significant step back since getting mentally ill. It felt like a personal victory that I could go to a new country by myself, and it made me feel like I could travel anywhere alone afterwards. I became completely comfortable with just approaching people on my own and striking up a conversation.

The next adventure would begin only a couple of weeks after I got home, so it was time to start getting excited about Sri Lanka. I borrowed a friend's backpack – you know, those massive ones that people take on their gap years (even though this was only technically a two-week holiday, not proper "travelling").

This trip was simply amazing, unlike any other I had been on before, and it made me want to visit more of Asia. The long flight there from Heathrow was an overnight journey, and I don't sleep well on planes. I ended up making a couple of friends and taking advantage of the free wine, which I later regretted when I arrived in Columbo quite tired and hungover.

One of the drawbacks of no longer being on medication was that it wasn't as easy to fall asleep. The medication can arguably make it too easy, and then you end up sleeping too much, but at least you don't have any trouble falling asleep. I think this trip was the first time that I struggled a bit with sleep, but it wasn't anything serious at this stage. (This was due to change in a couple of months, though.)

Sri Lanka was incredible. We had mostly sunny days but also some crazy heavy rain on a couple of occasions. The locals were all friendly and welcoming, and they spoke English, which was useful for us lazy Brits. We travelled round the island and did loads of exploring. There was a seven-hour train journey with amazing views, plus a few days of surfing in warm sea water, a safari trip featuring awesome elephants and so much more.

We met plenty of new people and made some nice friends. I can't recommend it enough as a location to visit. If you ever get the chance to go, definitely take it. I really loved the food there – even if some of it was too spicy for me – but I can't remember having a single bad meal.

When we got back home, I had an important event to look forward to. As previously mentioned, I had got in touch with the University of Hertfordshire about ways I could help as an alumnus, and they ended up asking me to visit the campus one day and do a little presentation about my mental illness experience. Even though I had already shared my experience through blogs and talking to others, this was a next-level experience. I had done presentations before, but never on this subject.

The event ended up being a really good experience for me. I was nervous, but really enjoyed it. The audience was only about 15 people in the end, so I wasn't too uncomfortable. Once I had told them the story of my illness and things that helped me recover, I received plenty of really nice feedback from the people who watched it. The presentation was also audio-recorded, so I was able to publish it via my YouTube channel.

Around this time I had also managed to get two more blog posts published, both for Trigger Publishing. The first one I have already shared in this book ("Mental Health at University"), and then I ended up doing a follow-up called "Mental Health After University." Here is a shortened version of the latter post:

# MENTAL HEALTH AFTER UNIVERSITY

Following on from my post about mental health at university, I wanted to cover another challenging time for young people: when you've graduated from uni, and it's time to face adult life.

So, you've had three or four incredible years of partying, living with your best mates, learning a subject that you're passionate about and loads more. Now it's time for some serious stuff in your 20s, like building a career and maybe trying to get on the property ladder (eventually). It's a completely different scene to uni, and it can seem difficult and daunting.

I want to cover some of the personal struggles I experienced at this point, as well as similar issues faced by people around me. However, the most important things I want to share are the positive lessons I've learnt on my journey – namely, how to overcome mental illnesses and maintain good mental well-being. So, here we go.

There's no doubt that after uni, life becomes completely different. I was living in a bubble at the University of Portsmouth for three years, then had a slightly more serious year doing a master's at the University of Hertfordshire. My next step was to do a ski season.

When I returned to the UK, I attempted and failed to get a job related to my degree in marketing. I got frustrated when I received no job offers from interviews. I was also temping at a market research agency at the time. They ended up offering me a permanent role, so I took it because I so desperately wanted any full-time job.

Back then I had started to put pressure on myself. I was too obsessed with earning money and I put this above doing a job I enjoyed. I ended up working in market research for the next four years. I wish that I hadn't chosen money over fulfilment. I'm not earning loads now, but I'm finally doing a job that makes me happy.

My first bit of advice is to pursue this too if you can. It's nice to use your degree in your job, but not necessarily essential. Loads of people don't work in the area they qualified in and are very content.

I think this makes a huge difference to mental health. I used to be stressed regularly in a corporate role that was going nowhere. Now I actually look forward to work at the end of the weekend, instead of having Sunday blues and dreading it.

We spend over 40 years in a career, so you might as well make it as good and enjoyable for you as it possibly can be! You might start off in a rubbish job, but it will give you the skills to get the next better job, as well as the motivation not to remain in an unfulfilled role. Always choose happiness over money. (A lot of rich people are miserable.)

Another difference from during and after uni might be the level of activity you're doing. Routines in full-time careers can become too samey: go to work, get home, have dinner, sleep and repeat. I've found that doing something either active or stimulating during the week or at the weekend, can make every week that much better.

Feeding your body well is also incredibly important. Don't deprive yourself, though – treats and fun times are needed, but so is body confidence, self-esteem and feeling good.

I've discovered all sorts recently, resulting in me losing nearly two stone in five months. In a nutshell: more fruit and veg, fibre and protein, less saturated fats and sugar. There are also plenty of tasty treats/healthy alternatives out there that are less naughty in moderation. Some of my favourites are dark chocolate, red wine, almond milk, black coffee, apples, butternut squash and bulgur wheat. (I could waffle on further about food too.)

In 2018, it's never been more essential to connect and communicate with people in person, especially when it comes to mental well-being. Spending more time away from phones and in company of close family and friends keeps me sane. I've been surprised at how supportive people can be when you open up about mental health. It also feels fantastic when you can support them back, and you feel honoured they choose you to confide in.

Have you ever heard the cliché, cheesy phrase that travelling "broadens the mind" and helps you "find yourself"? Well, it's not complete rubbish, ya know.

You don't have to go on a long, exotic and expensive trip, either. Seeing other places makes you appreciate your own home life. When you're away, I think living in the moment is the way forward.

Lastly, you could end up feeling really great mentally through volunteering or giving back to a charity cause or community. It's all about finding something that suits you – what are you passionate about and what makes you happy?

I guess I kind of got a bit keen on sharing my story and generally talking mental health at this point – maybe too keen and addicted, to an extent. I think I overdid it because it gave me a good feeling, and I was pursuing that feeling again. I decided to start a YouTube channel as a platform for sharing. I had some ideas for videos – I wanted to do one of my day at the Great South Run, and I also had a new project coming my way at work, which involved more paid hours and a chance to try something new. Looking back at these few months, I was starting to get a bit too busy and carried away with things, but I couldn't see it yet, and it would be a while before I realised where I went wrong.

# CHAPTER 14

# EARLY WARNING SIGNS

Firstly, let's talk about the weekend of the Great South Run. I had been training well and was very excited to take on a challenge that would involve running a distance I had not yet conquered. I was also looking forward to making a video of the experience. I had purchased a few bits to help with filming from my phone, including a selfie stick and a windscreen mount for filming myself driving. I had the idea of talking to the camera during my journey to Portsmouth.

The night before, I stayed over at my friend Dan's house in Basingstoke. I can't remember why, but I didn't sleep well at all the night before, probably partly due to excitement. I actually didn't sleep much at all, so ended up being over-tired for the day of the run.

I do cringe a bit thinking about my drive down to Portsmouth. Dan and I drove separately, as he was playing an ice hockey match near Portsmouth after the run – think he might have regretted that! Anyway, I am pretty sure I spent the entire journey down chatting absolute rubbish to my phone camera while driving. Luckily I am the only one who has re-watched (and deleted) most of the footage.

I was okay before and after the run, still filming bits and bobs but nothing too embarrassing, I think. The actual run went really well. It was an incredibly sunny and warm day for October, and the city where I spent three years at uni was looking great. The run was mostly enjoyable, apart from the last couple of miles (pain and struggle), but I managed to get a great time. We also met some people who worked for Mind at their stall; it was nice to speak to them about our fundraising.

The drive home was another cringe-fest when I think about my talking nonsense. I was literally just talking non-stop for most of the journey, as I was over-tired and probably a bit unwell. I think I was maybe on the verge of needing to be back on medication, but I was not self-aware enough to realise this. I did manage to sleep well that night and the following nights, so then, at least, I was still managing okay.

The end of October was the start date of this new work project that I previously mentioned. So, in addition to spending two days doing marketing for Groundwork East, I was now also working as a project assistant for them in Harlow. The project involved working with local volunteers who either had learning difficulties or mental health issues. We would be working with them for two days a week for eight weeks, and as a group we were gardening and carrying out horticulture-based tasks, including clearing overgrown gardens and local parks.

For me it was a helpful experience for many reasons. I was keen to help the volunteers with their mental health, self-esteem and confidence. They were all on Job Seeker's Allowance, and our project was a way for them to gain skills and experience that would hopefully help them get jobs. I also discovered that I really enjoyed the outdoor physical challenge of gardening, and found it to be very therapeutic and rewarding. Another reason I took on the job in the first place was to increase my chances of being offered full-time work with this charity, for which I had developed a great admiration.

The first few weeks of the project went really well, but it wasn't long before I realised the downside of what I was doing. Initially, I thought I would be able to cope and balance doing two part-time jobs. I did enjoy having the best of both worlds: having half my week in a relaxing office environment, then the other half immersed in the great outdoors doing gardening work. Eventually, though, it became a bit too overwhelming and too busy. I was starting to overdo it both physically and mentally.

I didn't help myself when I took on another two forms of "work" in October. Firstly, I discovered a charity in Luton (Bedfordshire), where someone who used to work for my charity was the fundraising and marketing manager. I reached out to her about volunteering for her as a fundraising assistant. I had seen some job roles advertised over the past few months that had "marketing" and "fundraising" in the job title. I thought that if I added some fundraising experience to my CV, this could further help me secure a full-time job in the industry. I volunteered for them one day per week, and found the role to be both enjoyable and interesting. So, at this point, I was effectively working three part-time roles.

Secondly, my cinema visits over the last few months had led to me discovering a great film podcast, which was hosted by two guys from Hemel Hempstead who were also Cineworld Unlimited members. I ended up meeting them one day, and it turned out they were looking for someone to help them grow the podcast through social media, so I offered to help them out.

I got along with them both really well, mainly due to the shared love of cinema, and at first I really enjoyed doing social media for them. The problem was, I was spinning too many plates at this point.

This was part of what led to me eventually having a blip with my mental health, which would happen in November.

Believe it or not, this was the same month I had said yes to yet another opportunity for a little holiday abroad! This time, a friend from Portsmouth was going to Milan with some of his family (his dad, uncle, their friends and his cousin), and extended the invite to the boys from uni.

So, I had another great trip to look forward to (trip number four in 2018), but I was not in a good place mentally. The annoying thing was, I still didn't really realise this myself!

In the meantime, following the success of my first Mind blog, I decided to do another one for them all about running and how it had helped me with well-being. You can find a link to the full post at the back of this book.

# CHAPTER 15

# THE BLIP

So, after all this great progress and a brilliant year so far, my blip was about to bring me crashing back down to earth. The main trigger was stress, caused by living my life with way too much going on and not taking a step back.

I had to take a week off work at one point. My stress ended up getting particularly high when I was in the process of buying travel insurance for the Milan trip. I was really annoyed at how high the prices were when I disclosed my mental health condition. My mum had to calm me down, as I was threatening to complain on Twitter and all sorts of silly things. I ended up taking the financial hit and agreeing with Mum that we would properly research travel insurance for next time. Admittedly, I had left it a bit last minute for this trip, but I still felt that the insurance provider was unfairly charging higher prices and discriminating.

The night before our flight, I ended up having another one of my terrible nights of virtually no sleep, probably from the stress of it all. I said to my friend Tommy on the way to the airport that he might have to look after me a bit. I tried to sleep on the plane but to no avail.

Despite my struggles, the trip was still really good. My behaviour was not always the best, though, and I had become a bit hyper. Luckily, I was in the company of the best of mates, who were able to look after me. By the end of the trip, one of them decided to text my mum to let her know that I was acting odd at times during the holiday. I was a bit annoyed when I first found this out, but eventually understood it was the right thing to do.

I ended up going to see a doctor from the community mental health team in Watford. After seeing me, he suggested that I should go back on the medication that I had been taking (aripiprazole). I told him that I was strongly against this, due to how it made me feel with its side effects. He said that I would be on a much lower dose this time, so this was very pleasing to hear. I decided to take his advice and go back on the meds, hoping it would not affect me so badly this time. He also put me on the waiting list for some cognitive behavioural therapy (CBT). I kept the letter that he sent to my GP and have included bits of it below:

29/11/2018

**Summary of appointment and current presentation:**
*Mr Lindsay attended an urgent medical review at Colne House on 29 November 2018. A senior associate practitioner was also present.*

*As you know, James stopped taking medication for his mental health, aripiprazole, in January of this year. He reports this has been a very good year. He was employed part-time by the charity in which he was volunteering, in Hatfield. He is doing marketing work and hopes to move to full-time hours. He really likes his employer, and they are very supportive towards him.*

*Concern was recently raised by his mother, who lives with him. She noticed he has become mildly excitable and more disorganised and distracted.*

*James said his sleep is normal, about 7/8 hours per night, except once a week when it is disturbed by his brother. He reported good mood most of the time, 8 or 9 out of 10. There was no evidence of elation or depression at the interview. He denied delusional ideas like delusions of reference he had when he was previously unwell. His thoughts are mildly racing when he is brainstorming at work, and tries to be creative. He reported good concentration when reading.*

**Mental state examination:**
*Well kempt, engaged well, with good eye contact and rapport.*
*Euthymic. No disorder or thought and perception. He was orientated in time, space and person. He has good insight into the previous episode of psychosis; he does not think he is relapsing at the moment.*

**Impression:**
*It is early to ascertain if James is relapsing into acute psychosis or not. At the moment medication is not indicated, but we offered monitoring and weekly engagement with the care coordinator to monitor his mental state for signs of early relapse. Path West will remain in contact with his mother with his consent, to collect collateral information and support her as a carer.*

**Risk review:**
- *Harm to self – low, denied suicidal ideas*
- *Self-neglect – low, no evidence of self-neglect*
- *Harm to others – low, no history or ideation*
- *Abuse by others – low*
- *Any risks to children – low*

**Recovery goals and actions:**
- *Weekly contact with our team*
- *Regular contact with his mother, to offer carer assessment and carer support group*

The drugs I was eventually prescribed helped me at first, as I gradually started to become calmer and less agitated. I had also realised by this point that my busy schedule was partly to blame, so I started to drop certain things.

I met up with my friend from the film podcast one Saturday morning for a parkrun. After the run, I told him that I had to take a step back from helping them, in order to prioritise my health. He completely understood, and was absolutely fine about it all.

I think around this time my whole "being headhunted" delusion came back to some extent. When I was having appointments at Colne House to see a psychiatrist or care coordinator, part of me thought that these were going to be secret meetings, and someone from a company was going to be there approaching me about an opportunity. I believe that, due to the success of the blogs I had published, my delusional thoughts were convincing me that organisations were tracking me and trying to reach out about working together. But as with the first time I had these thoughts in 2016, it was all in my head.

As far as work was concerned, there were only a few weeks left of the outdoor project anyway. Once that was over, I went back to having a relatively steady week. This was hard for me to do, because I had wanted to obtain a full-time job again for so long. The whole blip experience had a negative effect on both my confidence and self-esteem. I had come so far in recent months – it felt like such a setback.

December came, and it was a challenging month. At that point, I had been on the meds a little while, and unfortunately the side effects were back. I found myself having less energy, less motivation and less concentration.

I remember going out for a Christmas dinner with my friends from school. There were quite a lot of us there, and although I usually would really enjoy this type of occasion, I was just so tired. I had ordered a starter, main and dessert, but after the starters, I told my friends I had to go home. I was feeling terrible and not having a good time at all. I remember feeling devastated and holding back tears.

It was a very frustrating end to the year, but I was determined to get back on track.

As soon as I had the chance, I told my care coordinator and the doctor that the drugs and me were not getting along at all. They both tried to convince me to stay on them a bit longer, as did Mum. I politely explained that I could not possibly stay on them anymore – I was not going to let them ruin my life again.

The doctor eventually realised that these meds were a dead end, and he suggested an alternative medication, which I was open to trying. My diagnosis was also updated at this point. Before my condition was referred to as "acute polymorphic psychotic disorder with symptoms of schizophrenia". Now I was informed that my condition was called schizoaffective disorder.

The new drug I was prescribed was called quetiapine, another anti-psychotic. I really wanted this one to work for me, so I could reclaim life again and take back control. Despite the ending, 2018 had been a great year, and I desperately wanted 2019 to be just as good, if not better.

I did receive one really positive boost of good news in December, which I think I really needed at the time. A man called Liam who worked for Mind got in touch again. He was the one I had been liaising with about the first blog I did for them back in August, doing proofreads for me and providing suggested amendments before it got published. He emailed to inform me that the blog I wrote was first on their list of the most popular blogs of 2018.

I could not believe it! They did a little post on their website with the top five blog of the year and there I was.

Thankfully I am now over the worse of it and am currently living a much happier life.

— James

1. Blogs of the year    mind

I was so happy when I found out, and it was the best surprise ever. I was shocked, considering it got published in August, so it had less time to get page views than others published in January or February, for example. I saved his email as well for whenever I need a confidence boost.

*Hey James,*

*We're doing a little round up of our most popular blogs of the year, in terms of page views on the site. I'm sure you'll be pleased to know that yours was the most popular of the year, with over 15,000 people reading it. I'm sure it's helped a lot of people, so thanks so much again for sharing it.*

*Best wishes, Liam*

I was so delighted because I always say that if getting something like that published helps just one person, it will be worth it. The fact that more than 15,000 people read it still blows my mind, and this gives me so much motivation to continue writing. Part of my problem over the years has been focusing on the negatives and being overly critical of and hard on myself. I think it's important to try and overcome this way of thinking by regularly practising gratitude and remembering achievements big and small.

# MENTAL HEALTH PODCASTS

I love a good podcast; I have been obsessed with them for about a decade now. Over the years, I have discovered some really good ones that cover mental health. These are great for discovering new things that might improve your own mental well-being, or they can give you more peace of mind knowing that there are loads of people out there who are suffering with something similar. You should be able to find most of these on any podcast app – a quick Google search of the title will help you find up-to-date information as to the platform(s) playing these titles.

- *The VeryWell Mind Podcast* (with Amy Morin)
- *Happy Place* (with Fearne Cotton)
- *Mentally Yours*
- *The Joe Wicks Podcast*
- *Mental Health Foundation podcast*
- *I Weigh* (with Jameela Jamil)
- *Russell Kane's Man Baggage* (used to be called *Boys Don't Cry*)
- *I am. I have* (by *Happiful* magazine)
- *Under the Surface* (with Smithy and Marvin Sordell)
- *All Things Mental Health*
- *No Really, I'm Fine*
- *All in the Mind*

# CHAPTER 16

# DEPRESSION

After spending a few weeks on quetiapine, I realised that it was a much better match for me. There were still some small side effects, but they were nothing compared to what I had to put up with before. My mind felt a lot clearer, and I was not feeling tired all the time. I discovered that the side effects were minimal for most of the day, except the mornings when it felt a little more difficult to get out of bed, and also late in the evenings, but that part was actually convenient because it helped with falling asleep when I went to bed.

In January, my family and I attended a wedding up north in Cheshire. It was the daughter of my dad's best friend, who I had known pretty much my entire life. Thanks to the lack of side effects, I was able to enjoy a social occasion like this a lot more. I did discover that drinking alcohol caused the sedative effects of the meds to become more intense, but it was all manageable as long as I didn't have too much.

Meanwhile in my uni friends' WhatsApp group, another exciting adventure was on the horizon – yes, another one. This time, one of the lads suggested we join him on a trip to South America planned for May 2019, so five of the guys and I said we were well up for it. I think the idea was actually presented towards the end of the previous year, and around this time we had booked the flights. It definitely gave me something to look forward to, which I desperately needed.

My week now consisted of three to four days of work, a mixture of paid commitments and volunteering. I also started a beginner Spanish course at a local college, as I had heard that not many people speak English in South America, compared to other countries, anyway.

My mental health had been a bit up and down since my blip, but around this time it slowly became worse. My confidence was a bit all over the place, and I started to be quite hard on myself. I felt that I wasn't doing good enough in terms of my career, and that I should have a full-time job. I was once again doing that dangerous thing of comparing myself to others. I was frustrated I was living with parents, while most of my friends were in good jobs and had their own properties that they shared with long-term partners.

I started to become so worried about the future that I got myself quite worked up at times. I feared that I wouldn't always have someone to look after me; I thought I might become a lonely old man with nothing to show for his life.

I was having regular meetings with my care coordinator, who luckily was very good at her job and able to help me a lot − I felt a little bit more positive after a session with her. Sadly, the optimism was very short-lived, and I would find myself feeling really down again.

During my next doctor's appointment, I explained that I was feeling low all the time, and he agreed that I was experiencing depression. The doctor prescribed me a type of anti-depressant called sertraline, which is one of the selective serotonin reuptake inhibitors (SSRIs). I was much keener to be on this, as I knew I needed the help. I was still on a waiting list for CBT as well, which could not come soon enough.

I think depression is one of the hardest illnesses to overcome. I am pretty sure this was the second time I was depressed during the two previous years. In 2017 when I was jobless, I would go to bed dreading the next day, thinking there was nothing to look forward to. Then the next morning I would stay in bed until at least 11am, thinking, "What is the point of getting up? There is nothing to get out of bed for."

The second time in 2019 was equally as hard. I remember randomly bursting into tears at home because I was so sad. One weekend I went on a hike with Dan around the beautiful Virginia

Water area. It was such a nice day but I was too down to appreciate all the gorgeous nature around me. I struggled to make conversation during the walk because I didn't know what to say other than how fed up I was. When we were saying goodbyes, I even apologised for being so negative, as I felt like I was ruining the occasion. Dan was really nice about it and supportive – it helped having a friend I could lean on. When I drove home afterwards, I got emotional as a sad song came on the radio. (I think it was "Someone You Loved" by Lewis Capaldi.) I just completely erupted in floods of tears, feeling so sorry for myself.

I discovered a really good quote around this time that still stays with me to this day. It was during one of my many trips to the cinema, and I was seeing a film called *Beautiful Boy* starring Steve Carrell and Timothée Chalamet. It's a really powerful movie about a teenage boy and his addiction to meth. The quote was simply, **"Relapse is part of recovery."** This ended up giving me enormous comfort because I had naively assumed my recovery from psychosis was going to go one way. I hadn't considered that there would be setbacks, speedbumps, whatever you want to call them. I realised and began to accept that relapses (big or small) were sometimes an inevitable part of the process for some people, and that was okay.

In February things seemed like they were slowly improving, as I was finally able to find some more paid work. This was a temp role for a different charity based in Watford, so at least it was more local to where I was living. The role was three days per week, so I was able to do it alongside my other job, which was at that point two days a week. I was pleased that I was finally up to five paid days a week, but I was anxious that once again I had the challenge of balancing two different jobs, something that had overwhelmed me the last time I tried it. I was determined to make this one work, and I had the option of opting out if I wanted to, as it was a temp role and had no notice period.

But when I started this role, I received a piece of information that greatly concerned me. The lady who had been doing the job before and who I assumed would carry on as my line manager, was leaving the charity in just three weeks. This meant there was a short handover period, after which I would be left on my own.

My time there started off okay, but the worry about being alone soon kept growing. Eventually, after two weeks, I decided to quit due to the sheer amount of stress I was putting on myself. My care coordinator at the time said that I should put my health first, and was a temp job really worth all the hassle?! Looking back, I think I made the right decision, as I was then able to have a much more manageable weekly workload while I slowly tried to regain my confidence and improve my mental health.

Unfortunately, I had also recently dropped the Spanish lessons, as they would have clashed with the temp job. I did contact the tutor, but she made me realise that I would have been quite behind if I had re-joined the class. So, I decided once again to put health first. I thought trying to catch up with the Spanish had the potential to be stressful, and I was trying my best to make my life as stress-free as possible.

As well as having South America to look forward to, I also had an upcoming stag party on the horizon. One of my friends from school, Adam, was getting married in June, and his stag was in April. His best men had organised a few nights in Prague, Czech Republic.

Under normal circumstances, I would be really looking forward to these two trips abroad. I was sadly not myself at this point, however, so I was starting to dread the occasions. I viewed myself as a sad, depressed person who had nothing much to contribute or be proud of. I had actually fallen back into an old habit of my teenage anxiety, where I was imagining worst possible outcomes and scenarios before anything had even happened.

I was desperately trying to pull myself together, but not making much progress. I was living life on a kind of autopilot. When I saw people, I would put on a brave face and pretend things were okay, but inside I was scared and anxious all the time.

Fortunately, some help was soon on its way: my first CBT appointment was finally scheduled for early April. It could not come soon enough – I needed the help more than ever.

# CHAPTER 17

# DEALING WITH MENTAL ILLNESS ON A DIFFERENT CONTINENT

My first CBT appointment seemed promising. The therapist was a girl who looked around my age, and straight away I found her easy to talk to. The timings of the appointments were affected, however, by my travel plans. I was not able to make my second appointment due to being in Prague, so it had to wait until I was back.

I should mention that not long after being prescribed my two medications (I was now on quetiapine, an anti-psychotic, and sertraline, an anti-depressant), I had decided that I was not going to consume any alcohol for the time being. There were enough chemicals in my body for my liver to process – I was not going to take any risks by adding beer to the equation.

This, of course, made a stag party in Prague a bit of a unique experience. Luckily, another one of the guys was on meds for different reasons, so he was also keeping booze to a minimum. This made me feel a lot better about being surrounded by a drunk group of lads for most of the time there!

The trip turned out to be a lot of fun, and none of my previous catastrophising came to fruition. The nights out were still good, and I did find it amusing watching poor Adam having to do all sorts of silly things. The first night they made him wear a Luton FC top. (He is an avid Watford FC fan, so he would never normally be seen in colours of the local enemy.) Another night he had to go out dressed in an adult diaper/nappy, and, of course, they made him do plenty of shots and things like that. It turned out that every bar we went to offered at least one type of alcohol-free beer, and some of them were pretty tasty too.

So, I got back to the UK, and it felt like a bit of an achievement having survived a small getaway in Europe. When you are riddled with anxiety, depression or both, it can feel impossible to do certain things that may seem like nothing to some people. I was still really worried about going to South America, but I had at least proved to myself that I was capable in some capacity of leaving home for a while.

I had one more CBT session before going away again. This process was still in the very early stages, and having those two trips close together caused a disruption and made it difficult for the therapy to have much effect. Despite this, I did take some comfort in the fact that the process had at least started and would be there to finish when I got back.

So, the time came for the big adventure to begin. I had received all of the various injections needed, including the yellow fever jab. I had got myself a massive backpack, plenty of suitable clothes, sun cream, insect repellent, local currencies – I had everything I physically needed.

Mentally, on the other hand, I could have done without all the anxiety, and could have done *with* some more confidence. But I wasn't going alone. My travel companions were five of my best friends from uni – Dan, Tom, Jack, Josh and Hinesh – who I had known for more than ten years and been on adventures with before (for example, Sri Lanka with Jack and Tom the previous year). I knew that they would be there for support if I needed it, and that gave me great comfort and some much needed peace of mind.

As with Prague, I had built up a number of things to worry about in my head. Would I get unwell from food? Would I injure myself or fall off a cliff? Would it all be too much and give me a mental breakdown? The list went on.

The flight from Heathrow was a very long one. This time, unlike Sri Lanka, where I had too much airplane alcohol, I tried my best to get a good sleep. I am terrible at sleeping on planes and I didn't get much, but it was better than nothing.

Our first stop was Bogotá in Columbia, where we arrived at the hostel in the early hours of the morning. Then, as a group, we decided to explore the area, which included a pretty epic hike up a mountain not far from where we were staying. I was still in pretty decent shape from getting into so much exercise and sport the year before and had carried on doing a lot of it in 2019, including the parkruns. I still found the uphill hike very hard, but it was all worth it – we had spectacular views of Bogotá from the very top and took loads of pictures (like the one on the next page).

In the evenings, I was sticking to my "no booze" rule, despite the fact that I could not seem to find anywhere that served zero-alcohol beers. We only spent one night in Bogotá; our next stop was Medellin where we had two nights planned. This turned out to be a brilliant city, and I really enjoyed my time there: plenty of cool places and I felt safe the whole time. There were loads of really cool bars and restaurants, so we enjoyed plenty of good local food as well.

I did begin to get a bit frustrated, though, as it turned out that none of the places that we went served alcohol-free beers. I was getting fed up with colas and lemonades, and increasingly jealous of the nice-looking drinks the guys were enjoying. One night, I decided to experiment and see how a little bit of alcohol would make me feel. I assured my friends I was going to be careful and take it slow.

The first night I did this, it turned out fine. I had a couple of beers while we enjoyed playing card games at our hostel, then woke up the next morning feeling good. The trouble was that this made me think I could handle even more. The next night, I had a bit more to drink, and again it felt pretty much how it used to before I was on meds. That was our last night in Columbia, and the next morning we got on a flight to Lima, Peru. So far so good – but it wasn't long before I took things a bit too far.

# CHAPTER 18

# OUTSIDE OF MY COMFORT ZONE

In Lima we stayed in another hostel, and this one had a different vibe from the others. Up until this, the places had been fairly chilled and quiet, but now there was more of a louder party atmosphere, since everyone staying there was fairly young.

We didn't mind this at all, and the drinks soon started flowing. The main socialising area was a rooftop with plenty of seating areas, table tennis tables and football tables. We had a really enjoyable first night and met a few fellow travellers, including plenty of tipsy table tennis players. This was the first time on the trip where I ended up getting quite drunk, which at the time didn't seem like a big deal, but it ended up massively disrupting my sleep over the next few nights.

The next day, we went on the most incredible excursion – we went on a boat trip to some nearby little rock islands, which were swarmed with hundreds of sea lions. It was an amazing sight to behold, then it was even better when the guides got the group to jump in the sea. We had to form a line with our arms locked and stick our legs out, almost like being in a seated position. The sea lions then slowly started inspecting our feet and getting up close to us. It was so much fun, and I was really glad we did it.

From the time I jumped in the sea and felt the cold water enveloping me until we got back on the boat, all my worries, depression, anxiousness, all of it, completely vanished. Even though it was only temporary, I felt more alive than ever. For me, it was an unforgettable life experience, and the perfect distraction from mental illness.

That evening, we had another good time at the hostel, but didn't get too carried away since we were leaving the next day to travel to our next destination, Cusco.

But that night, the worst possible thing happened: I could not fall asleep at all. So, I stayed awake the whole night and didn't even manage one hour.

Part of the reason for this was my increasing anxiety, as there was something that had been troubling me that got worse as the trip went on. I found it very stressful having to constantly re-pack and figure out which things I would need in my bag for the next day. It doesn't sound like much to some people, but my backpack only opened from the top, so sometimes I would have to take most of the contents out just to find one thing. I built this problem up in my head – I was, in some ways, making a mountain out of a molehill.

The next day I tried to sleep during the journey to Cusco, but was not able to. By the time we arrived, I was in a really bad way, and my friends noticed I was really quiet, really down and really anxious in general. So, the guys all chipped in to pay for a bed in a local hostel so that I could try and sleep for the afternoon. I was so grateful for that.

The others went out to explore, and I tried to sleep for the afternoon. Annoyingly, my over-tiredness was still not letting me fall asleep, but I was at least glad that I was generally resting and relaxing in a safe environment.

The plan was then to get dinner in town somewhere; then we had an overnight bus scheduled to take us to Bolivia, where we planned to stay for a few days to see the salt flats and go mountain biking at their famous "Death Road". The trouble was that these were also some of the things I had become anxious about too.

Back at the hostel after dinner, I remember phoning home and speaking to Mum. I did not want to get her upset, but I had to be honest about how I was feeling and that I was struggling. I was surprised that she said that if I really wasn't enjoying it, then she would pay for an early flight if I wanted to come home instead. As much as I didn't want her to spend the money on this, I really appreciated having that option available, and it did give me some comfort. We decided that I would see how I got on with the overnight bus, then let her know if I was going to stay.

After the call, I re-joined the guys. Jack asked me if I was okay, and I broke down in tears. I felt so overwhelmed and completely erupted with emotion.

They were really good about it, and I told them everything; we had a long chat, and they said they would help me out as much as they could. I felt lucky to be sharing the experience with such supportive friends. And I felt really glad that I was not there alone – I was in such a state of anxiety, I dread to think what would have happened to me if I was on my own. Even if I got the early flight home, making that actually happen and doing that journey by myself would have been terrifying and maybe even traumatic.

We went to a supermarket to stock up on snacks for the journey, then got on the bus. It was more comfortable than most daytime buses I had been on, but it was essentially a "trying to sleep sitting upright" situation ahead of us.

I sat next to Jack, who told me to wake him up if I needed to chat or anything, which was so nice of him and made me feel at ease. We all put our eye masks on, and I put in my foam ear plugs, hoping I would finally get the sleep I needed.

# CHAPTER 19

# THE ADVENTURE OF A LIFETIME

Miraculously, I ended up having the best sleep I'd had on that bus!

I woke up feeling like a completely different person. I felt a million times better, and I actually experienced optimism and positivity for a change instead of dread and worry. We were having breakfast, and I messaged Mum saying that I was feeling really good compared to yesterday, and I that was determined to stay for the rest of the trip.

Thankfully, I had experienced a key turning point and was able to start enjoying myself again. We arrived in La Paz, Bolivia, and this time we were staying in a pretty decent hotel rather than a cramped hostel. I was more well-rested, shaved and showered, and I was not experiencing as much anxiety.

While we were in La Paz, something big was happening back home for my football team: Watford were playing Man City in the FA cup final at Wembley stadium, and we managed to find a bar that was showing the game. I was the only Watford fan there and was wearing my shirt with pride, hoping that we were going to win the first major trophy in our history.

The game could not have gone worse. I was glad not to be back home at Wembley, as I watched us lose the match 6-nil! It was quite embarrassing in the end, but that is football sometimes.

The next day we travelled to the Bolivian Salt Flats, and I was absolutely blown away by the place. It was like nothing I had ever seen before – it was almost like being on a completely different planet (minus the lack of gravity you'd get in space). I would go as far to say that it's possibly the best area I have ever visited. The views are the most stunning and beautiful you can imagine, it's hard to believe it exists. We took LOADS of pictures. We did a human pyramid shot, jump-in-the-air shots, giant-and-small-person shots... all sorts of silly stuff, and we had so much fun.

A couple of days later, we took on the challenge of mountain biking down the infamous "Death Road". I wasn't the only one who was a little scared of doing this, but there was at least a minibus with us the whole time as an alternative to biking. I tried to keep up with Dan at the very start of the descent and ended up falling off the bike straight away. This shook me up a little bit and affected the rest of my ride, but it was still a very thrilling experience. The views were breath-taking, and it didn't feel as dangerous as we first thought. There were several beautiful waterfalls along the route, some of which we even got to cycle under. The cold waterfall was a nice relief, as it was very hot and humid! Some of the route was very bumpy and ended up giving me a lot of pain in my hands and wrists, so when we were nearly at the bottom, I decided to get in the bus.

At the end of the ride, there was a swimming pool and a bar where we enjoyed well-earned food and a beer together. I had learnt my lesson by this point to keep the booze in moderation. I was glad I had the choice to enjoy a drink while on medication, but I was now very self-aware and more sensible about my choices.

A few days later was the last of our epic excursions, and one we had all been looking forward to. We had travelled back to Cusco, Peru, but this time we decided to get a flight there rather than overnight bus. We all didn't mind spending a bit more money, as it meant getting there quicker and without as much discomfort.

We were back in Peru to hike the Inca Trail that leads to Machu Picchu. I have done plenty of hikes in my time, but this has to be one of my all-time favourites. It was hot, intense and difficult, but very much worth it. The environment surrounding us was the greenest of green, and the surrounding views were immense. Our tour guide was excellent as well. He stopped loads of times to show us all sorts of wacky and wonderful things, including funnel-web spiders – Google them!

We made it to Machu Picchu, and it was a marvellous sight to behold. The only slight downside was the sheer number of tourists that were there – it was more crowded than I was expecting. This did not matter, though; I was at a truly epic place and loving life.

I paused for a moment and appreciated that I was there. I had been well out of my comfort zone on parts of this trip, but it was worth it, and I was starting to feel proud of myself for not going home and deciding to face my fears.

It had been the adventure of a lifetime, and I highly recommend South America as a destination. My only regret was not learning more Spanish. Luckily, Josh was there to be our translator when we needed him, and I was really impressed at how well he was able to speak and understand the language. He had clearly had plenty of lessons, and seemed to keep getting better the more we were there.

A few days later it was time to return to England, and I was feeling very relieved to be going back to home comforts. I had survived the trip that I was previously dreading, I had overcome a lot, and I returned to the UK with a renewed sense of purpose. I was looking forward to getting my life back on track and was going to try my best to finish the year strongly.

# MENTAL HEALTH BOOKS

I know I have already mentioned books, but I wanted to put a full list together of books I recommend that have helped me over the years. If it wasn't for reading someone else's mental health story, I would never have found the courage to start talking about my own experiences. What I like about books is that they are your own private experience, and are often a good stepping stone for someone who is still not feeling comfortable about opening up, like I was. You can discover books at your own time and pace, and the best part is using your own imagination as you are reading them. Here are some fantastic books I have read, which I think fully deserve recognition:

- *Mad Girl* by Bryony Gordon
- *Reasons to Stay Alive* by Matt Haig
- *Maybe I Don't Belong Here* by David Harewood
- *Let Me Be Frank* by Frank Bruno
- *Happy* by Fearne Cotton
- *I Used to Be a Miserable F*ck* by John Kim
- *One Flew Over the Cuckoo's Nest* by Ken Kesey
- *Bring Me to Light* by Eleanor Segall
- *The Stranger on the Bridge* by Jonny Benjamin and Britt Pflüger
- *Jog On* by Bella Mackie

# CHAPTER 20

# BACK TO MY BEST SELF

Once my adventures abroad had come to a close, I could focus on myself again. This meant I was finally able to have a CBT session once every week for consecutive weeks, and I really started to feel and notice the whole point of it and what my therapist had been trying to accomplish the whole time.

I discovered that CBT was a highly effective form of treatment for me, and it turned out that I really benefitted from it. I think I cried in over half of my sessions, but I always came away from the appointment feeling better than when it started.

My therapist was really good and would draw all sorts of mind maps to help illustrate what she was talking about. We established that I was uncomfortable with uncertainty and I had a low opinion of my life so far. I was initially very hard on myself and would be overly critical of things like work.

She was able to make me realise that uncertainty is something to be embraced if you can manage it, rather than avoiding it. If I could become more comfortable with uncertainty and stressful situations, then it would help me a lot with everyday life going forward. She also helped me to appreciate being in the present more, and she always had lots of great analogies and metaphors to help explain things.

One of my favourites was the idea of treating yourself as your own best friend, or treating your own mind as a "friendly scientist". If your best mate was going through a hard time with mental illness, you would offer nothing but kindness and support, so why not do this to yourself? A friendly scientist would also be curious and intrigued by all the different thoughts and feelings our minds go through, rather than criticising or being harsh about them and jumping to conclusions.

I learnt a lot about myself during CBT, and at first it was challenging to change my way of thinking, which had been my default for most of my life. By the end of it (around August 2019), I had made so much progress. I would highly recommend it to anyone as a form of therapy.

Meanwhile, it was time for Adam's wedding (who had recovered from Prague by then). I had a great time at this event, partly because I was able to tell everyone how amazing South America had been. This was the first of many nice occasions during the summer, and I was able to really start enjoying my social life again now I was in a better place mentally.

At the end of June, I was able to get myself a job interview for a full-time marketing assistant role at a charity called National Animal Welfare Trust (NAWT). This was a big deal for me and was the type of work I had been pursuing for so long – for well over a year at that point, in fact.

I managed to get through to their second interview stage in July, which included writing a blog post about one of their animals.

The following week, I was out volunteering for Groundwork East. We were doing a garden clearance job, and it was a nice hot sunny day. I remember really vividly getting the call from NAWT offering me the job, and I was so delighted! All the hard work through volunteering, temping, etc., had paid off, and I finally had the type of job that I'd had in mind when I did my degree.

The rest of the summer was full of good times. I had become fitter and active again and was enjoying all kinds of things that were helping my overall well-being: yoga, parkruns, football, seeing friends, cinema, reading. I even tried some local dance classes, as I heard they were meant to be really good for the brain. I felt brave going to these alone, and I would never have had the confidence to go before!

In August, I started the new job, and there were so many things to love about working for NAWT. Two of the head office team would bring their dogs to work every day, so I would be giving them plenty of fuss in between sending emails. I found the work really enjoyable and was able to use my creativity and writing skills on a daily basis. Plus, posting pictures of cute cats on social media never got old!

Working in animal welfare turned out to be great for my dating apps around this time too. I was also feeling in a great place as a person, which helps massively when you are trying to find that special someone for a relationship. I had been single for over three years at that point, and even though I was appreciating the lifestyle at times, the ultimate goal was to find the real thing again. I now had the career and social life I wanted; the next aims were moving out and getting a girlfriend.

September included a great camping holiday in the Peak District with a bunch of the guys from uni, as well as the first of many 30th birthday parties from the school and uni circles. Then, in mid-October, something really wonderful happened.

# CHAPTER 21

# LOVE COMES BACK AROUND

Holly and I started talking on the dating app Hinge. She lived near Watford and was working for British Airways as cabin crew. We hit it off straight away, and it was not long before we arranged our first date: drinks at a pub not far from where I was living. I liked how she was happy to meet me there, despite it being further away from her and closer to me – a great first impression!

The date could not have gone better. We had a lot in common, and there was plenty of laughter! She even gave me a lift home in her car, which was nice, although I kept forgetting to give her directions because we were chatting away so much. When we arrived outside my house, we had our first kiss, and it wasn't long before date number two was arranged.

It happened the very next day, in fact. I already had plans to go to the cinema on my own, but I decided to invite her along and get dinner before as well. I then ended up seeing her another two times the same week!

By the end of October, I realised that this was turning into something really special. I had not felt this way about a girl since my last relationship. We were spending lots of time together and were falling for each other really quickly.

In early November, I asked her to be my girlfriend. Things were moving pretty fast, but it all just felt so right.

One weekend, my family and I were going out for a birthday meal for my mum and dad (both of their birthdays are in early November), so I invited Holly along to meet my parents and brother. It was a great evening, and she clicked with them straight away. Plus, she also ended up meeting Adam, because we had booked a table at the pub/restaurant where he was the manager.

Later that month, I was also able to introduce her to a lot of my friends from both school and university. Things were going so well, and I was delighted that we had met. I was feeling really content and complete as a person by this point. The new job was going great, and now I was also very much in love – the year 2019 was certainly ending on a high!

Since Holly worked for an airline, she had been lucky enough to travel to a lot of places around the world. This initiated plenty of conversions between us about travelling and areas we would love to visit. Then, one day at the end of November, we decided to book ourselves a little holiday together to Cologne, Germany, for early December. We were both keen to experience all the wonderful Christmas markets that we had heard about from friends.

We stayed at a very nice Airbnb when we got there, which was located quite centrally in Cologne and within walking distance of the Christmas markets. The markets themselves were brilliant, and we enjoyed loads of great local food and drinks. We had a lovely time there together, and I would definitely recommend Cologne as a place to visit if you can.

We got back to the UK, and Christmas time was just around the corner, but little did I know that something else was coming that would affect my life in a really horrible way.

Up until this point, my mental health was stable, and I was taking 100mg per day of the antipsychotic medication quetiapine. My regular box of tablets contained 100mg per tablet, so all I had to do was take one pill every evening.

Frustratingly, a very important detail was missed following our next visit to the pharmacy. My mum offered to pick up my next round of pills because she was also getting some for my dad. The pharmacist gave Mum my tablets, but these were 50mg pills that I was supposed to take twice daily, instead of my usual once-a-day 100mg tablets. The pharmacist did not point out this important detail, nor did Mum or I notice the different label.

I carried on taking my one tablet per day, completely oblivious to the fact that I was only taking 50mg, HALF of my dosage. Things were about to get a lot worse very quickly.

# CHAPTER 22

# RELAPSE

One week during mid-December, I ended up having a very hectic few days. I was driving to Berkshire one morning to visit the local NAWT centre and meet some of my colleagues from this area. I stopped at a service station for a coffee and checked my work messages.

My manager had let me know that she had to edit one of my published social media posts because I had made a couple of errors. She was not having a go at me, and her tone was not negative or critical, but I completely overreacted to this and got very angry at myself. The rest of journey I spent overanalysing the situation and telling myself off, so I got into a bit of state.

The centre visit itself was fine, and I ended up meeting my friend Dan for dinner on the way home, since he lived not far away from my route. This helped me calm down and relax a bit, but this was to be the first of many instances where my mind started to get out of control.

It didn't help that, around this time, my sleep started to decline to alarming levels. By the weekend, I had gotten much worse, and Mum decided that we needed to get me urgent help.

I remember Mum and Dad were supposed to be visiting my nan that weekend. She was in her 90s and lived at a care home near Brighton, not far from where my aunt and uncle lived. My parents ended up cancelling their trip because my behaviour was becoming far too concerning.

This time, things were worse than when I had a blip the year before – I was having a full-blown relapse. Psychosis had reared its ugly head once again.

I am not sure why or where it came from, but I had become convinced that my nan had passed away and became really upset. I was crying into Holly's shoulder, and it was distressing for her to see me like this for the first time. My mum ended up taking me to A&E at Watford General Hospital, just as she had been forced to do three years earlier when I'd had my first psychotic episode.

As was the case with the first episode, my memory of this period isn't the best. So, I decided to sit down with Holly and get her perspective, since she was spending the most time with me, alongside my family.

## CONVERSATION WITH HOLLY

**James:** "What are your first memories of the time when I started having the relapse and becoming ill again, in terms of warning signs?"

**Holly:** "I must admit that your mum noticed it more than I did because she had witnessed it before. But the first sign was when I was staying at yours. I was asleep, and around 3am, you turned the main bedroom light on."

**James:** "Oh dear, really?! I would never normally do that."

**Holly:** "Yeah, so, I was like, 'What are you doing, what's going on?' You said you couldn't sleep, and you were going downstairs to play PS4 and asked if I wanted to join you."

**James:** "I don't know why I thought you would join me."

**Holly:** "I said, 'No, I would rather not, can you turn the light off, please?' So, you went downstairs by yourself. Then, the next day, we were meant to go and see your Nan, but your mum said she didn't think you were well enough to go. You got really angry, but I naively thought you were fine."

**James:** "I am pretty certain I would not have had any sleep at that point, so I would have been in a bad way. Also, I still can't believe I turned the light on during the night."

**Holly:** "I know, because what you usually do is quietly leave the room and read a book or play PS4 if you can't sleep. You wouldn't turn the light on and ask me to join."

**James:** "I do remember the day after fairly well because, for some reason, I don't know how or why, but I had it in my head that Nanny had passed away when actually she hadn't."

**Holly:** "Yeah, you were running up and down the stairs because you couldn't find your dad. He was getting changed or getting ready. And you were checking everyone was okay. I believe your mum eventually was able to convince you that your nan was fine. But you were worried about everyone in the house and running everywhere trying to check everyone was okay."

**James:** "I think this was the same day that I went to A&E, right?"

**Holly:** "It was, yeah. Your mum took you there, and I had to go home."

**James:** "What was I like the day after I went to A&E?"

**Holly:** "You apologised for what you put us through the day before and said that you were fine now. I remember thinking you might be okay, but then realised a couple of minutes later that you weren't."

**Holly:** "We were in your bedroom, and you kept showing me random things that were not making sense, and you were jumping from one subject to another. I couldn't keep up."

**James:** "That's something I was doing the first psychotic episode as well."

**Holly:** "Yeah, and I couldn't understand you. At one point you had this plastic tube that was one of those tennis ball holders, but you had filled it with all this other random stuff. I don't know why you did it, and you kept showing me it like you were proud of it, and you kept trying to tell me what it was, but I don't think even you knew what it was."

**James:** "I don't remember this at all."

**Holly:** "I was feeling a bit upset because I couldn't believe that I thought you were okay at first."

**James:** "Do you know what I had put in the tennis tubes?"

**Holly:** "Honestly, I am not sure, I was just trying to go along with it. I didn't want to make you feel stupid or frustrate you or anything like that. You were very excitable, so I was just trying to calm you down, really."

This time, thankfully, my condition was not as severe as the first time, and I was not sectioned again – thank God. I had various doctors' appointments, and my medication was increased. I also had a recommendation to be registered with a nearby mental health centre in Hemel Hempstead.

This was called an acute day treatment unit (ADTU), and it was a place where people can go voluntarily to get their mental illness treated. The staff there offered all sorts of individual and group therapy sessions, and this was to become something I would have to get used to.

It was a really difficult way to end the year for me. I had made so much good progress, and it felt like it had all come crashing down.

My average week became very different, as I was not going to work; instead, I was spending around three days of the week at the ADTU. This was a very mixed experience. I met plenty of people there who were going through similar illnesses as me, and the group therapy sessions were hit and miss. The main difference between the first episode and the relapse was that I was angry all the time during the latter.

I am never usually an angry person, but in early 2020, I had so many outbursts. I feel terrible, as a lot of them were aimed at my family who were only trying to help me. I remember getting very wound up and aggressive at my Wednesday afternoon football sessions. I would get way too competitive and start having a go at my team if they weren't defending or passing. I'm sure I was very unpleasant to be around at the time. The guys who ran the football were helpful and spoke to me separately, and they spoke to Holly and my mum when they were picking me up at the end of the sessions too.

There was plenty of unusual behaviour from me around this time as well. One of the things I remember doing was posting pictures and videos on my WhatsApp groups and on social media, which were just completely random, had no context and made no sense. They probably had some meaning to my damaged mind at the time, but I am sure anyone else who viewed them would be thinking, "What the hell was that all about?"

I also did this weird thing of going through old WhatsApp groups on my phone – groups that had ran their course and were no longer needed, or groups that people had already exited or deleted. I would leave random comments or pictures in these groups which, again, were just complete nonsense. I guess part of me was so bored from not going to work, but I would not normally do this and was not my regular self.

In fact, at one point, one of my uni friends actually removed me from our boys WhatsApp group. He messaged me straight after and reassured me that it was only because my recent messages were concerning, and he would add me back as soon as I was on the mend. I appreciate him doing this, even if at the time I was pretty devastated, but it had to be done, and it was the right thing.

There were some nights when I wasn't able to get much sleep, and I ended up behaving very bizarrely. I am glad that no one else was around to witness these moments, and I am embarrassed to even write about them. I must emphasise that I was very unwell at this point and would not usually do anything like this. One night, after trimming my beard, I convinced myself through my delusion that if I ingested some of the hair that I had trimmed off, it would help more hair grow on the top of my head, where it was lacking. I still can't believe I did it, but I actually ate some bloody hair – it was revolting. Another night, I convinced myself that I could improve my hair and skin not by eating a banana, but by crushing it in my hands and applying it on my face and head. What a waste! I was covered in banana for a few minutes before deciding to wash it all off. I haven't told anyone about these incidents because they are the unwell version of me. I am just glad they only happened once, and no one actually saw me doing them.

In February, I went on a weekend trip to Somerset with loads of friends from uni to celebrate the 30th birthdays of three people in the group. I really enjoyed this trip, but some parts of it make me cringe because of my illness. One night we were doing karaoke at the house we were staying in, something in which I would not normally participate, but I got carried away. I remember singing my heart out and really going for it in front of the group. I really hope none of them filmed it – or if they did, I hope they deleted the video – because I definitely can't sing, and I am sure the whole thing was just really awkward and embarrassing. I was acting out of character, and this was obvious to everyone.

I was so hyper and talking rapidly to such an extent that whenever I went round to Holly's house or she came to mine, she would get me to do a meditation before we did anything else, just to try and calm me down. This would sometimes help, but other times it just effectively paused my rambling. At least it gave her a bit of a chance to relax before having to cope with my relentless energy.

My medication kept getting increased, but my condition was not improving very much. Mum, Holly and I began to get a bit frustrated with the whole process and started to question whether I was on the right drug. Maybe it was time to try something new.

Things were getting so bad, and at one point, I had a little scare where I thought Holly was going to break up with me. To be honest, I would not have blamed her if she did, as I was just so difficult to tolerate at the time. I ended up writing her a heartfelt, handwritten letter and dropping it off at her house. I promised her that I was going to focus on getting better and make up for all the shit I had put her through since having my relapse.

In March, my meds were increased for a final time to see if this would make a difference before trying an alternative. At long last, I started to become stable and started heading in the right direction. It had been a horrible three months, but now we could all see the light at the end of the tunnel.

Of course, we all know what happened in March 2020. Just as I was starting to get my life back at last, the UK was put into lockdown due to the Covid-19 pandemic.

# CHAPTER 23

# POST-PSYCHOSIS PANDEMIC

The next few months were unlike anything I had experienced before. I hated lockdown! My favourite hobbies, such as going to the cinema, were shut down, so I found myself going out for the longest walks just for something to do. I watched a lot of Netflix and played a lot of PS4, but my return to work was delayed again and again due to bloody Covid.

I had time on my hands – maybe too much time – but one of the positives of this was that I was able to get another two blogs published.

The first that came out was in April for the University of Hertfordshire. I had decided to get in touch with their alumni team and managed to get featured on their "Alumni Stories" website section, which was a really satisfying way to give back to the university that had given me such a good experience. You can read my post about coping with my mental health during the Covid-19 pandemic through the link at the back of the book.

Then, not long after, I was able to see the finished version of my third blog for Mind, which got published in May. These two were both a welcome boost amongst a bleak and boring lockdown. The Mind blog was about my relapse and how the Man On! program has helped me over the years. I have included a shortened version of my blog below, and you can find a link to the full version at the back of the book.

# HOW FOOTBALL HAS HELPED ME THROUGH RELAPSES AND COVID-19

On World Mental Health Day last year (10 October 2019), the Premier League released a video of me. That sentence sounds ridiculous as I write this, but let me explain how my mugshot ended up alongside famous footballers on Google search.

Exercise has helped me a lot since suffering my first psychotic episode back in September 2016. It's now over three years since I had that first full psychotic breakdown, resulting in me being sectioned.

Football has been a regular form of my weekly exercise since primary school. My enjoyment of playing and watching it has gone up and down over the years, but things changed once I discovered that one of my local charities was offering 90-minute sessions on a 4G AstroTurf near where I live and work.

Over the summer last year, I started participating in a project called Man On!, a football session in Watford aimed at men aged 18–65 who have experienced mental health difficulties.

And so, on Saturday 5 October, I was interviewed, then shadowed by a film crew, as I trained with my Man On! teammates and played a friendly against FC Not Alone at our pitch in Watford.

We then went to Vicarage Road Stadium to watch Watford FC play against Sheffield United in their Premier League fixture. I was filmed outside, then inside the stadium. Other fans were jumping in front of the camera thinking they were getting on live television. I felt like a fake celebrity being followed around by a cameraman – it was such a bizarre yet cool experience!

I probably come across in the video a bit more confident than how I am in person. This is thanks to amazing national charities like Mind, who are always supporting people like me with mental illness. On the day, I tried my hardest playing football, as well as watching it with the friends I've made through the Man On! team. I wore my heart on my sleeve and thought of all the brave professional football players who have inspired me over the years (for example, Watford captain Troy Deeney).

When you have a strong support team of family and friends behind you, it can give you the determination you need not only to help yourself, but to encourage others to share their mental well-being. I felt so good about what I was doing.

When the filming was over, I was relieved, as it was a little stressful, but it was well worth doing for the cause. The match we all watched ended 0–0, which was a shame as Watford FC needed the win, but nothing could change the positive buzz I had about this day, which I will certainly never forget.

The day the video got released on the Premier League website and Twitter was incredible. I was with the Man On! gang that day too, playing in the National Mental Health Football Championships near Liverpool.

At this tournament were groups just like us, all very friendly and approachable, how football should be! We lost every game, sadly, but I managed to score a goal and our goalkeeper Mark received the "keeper of the tournament" trophy. To me, that felt like a massive win! I have to admit that I was also a bit distracted that day after the online video was released. I remember showing it to my teammates briefly between matches, then I had to get my concentration back on taking part in the tournament.

The camaraderie of being part of a football team has been particularly important for me recently. In December last year, I unfortunately had to go through another relapse, caused by a mistake in taking my medication.

Thankfully, after a few months of recovering under the care of a specialist mental health team in Hertfordshire, I am feeling back on track and ready to resume everyday life. I was still playing football with the guys every Wednesday during my recent recovery. The sessions have become like therapy to me!

I believe that sport can be excellent for mental well-being when it is done right. I feel like I can talk to any of the Man On! guys about my mental health; we share things every week and it feels good. As well as the benefits of opening up about my mental health with the group, physical exercise helps release endorphins and serotonin, which makes me feel fantastic.

I firmly believe that football, for some people, is a universal language, and it brings people together from all walks of life. I am determined, now more than ever, that my recent relapse is going to be my last. I think playing football and sharing my ups and downs will play a key part in maintaining good mental health in the future.

For some people, though, it's not all about just football, which is fair enough. I would advise anyone to try all sorts of sport and exercise, then pick the ones that boost your mental health the most.

One of my takeaways from the pandemic experience is that, looking back, it doesn't seem real, as if it is some weird dream. I feel like, in another universe, the virus never happened, and they are watching a film/programme about what we are going through.

The brighter side of lockdown was that I was stable, and my mental health was back on track. I did plenty of gardening, running and volunteering while I was waiting to return to work, which finally happened in June. I started by working from home for two days per week, then gradually did more hours as the weeks went on.

In July, I joined the 30 club! I couldn't have a proper birthday party, but we were able to organise a nice picnic in the park with my family and some local friends. Looking back on my 20s, there were many highs, but also a lot of struggles with mental illness. I decided that my 30s were going to be different. I had learnt to look after my mental well-being and was determined to use the knowledge to better myself and have the best possible life.

Restrictions were eased by August, and I was able to enjoy cinema visits again, thank God! However, it wasn't long before Covid-19 cases started shooting up again, and we had lockdown 2.0.

Holly and I managed to end the year on a high by having a little staycation in Portsmouth and Isle of Wight in December. Plus, by that point, we had done a flat viewing for a place in Bushey (near Watford). Our plan was to live together in rented accommodation for a year before looking for somewhere to buy, so we had that to look forward to!

I was looking at the year 2021 full of optimism. Holly and I moved into our flat in January, which was really exciting. I had also seen that the charity who ran my Man On! football sessions were advertising their London Marathon place for October. I sent off my application for this, as the marathon had always been on my bucket list. At the end of the month, I found out I got the place! It was time to buy some new running shoes and get training.

When I was a kid, I remember watching the London Marathon on TV in the morning. I would boldly proclaim that, one day, that would be me! So, to have the chance to do it myself was very exciting.

Initially the marathon training was doing me a lot of good – it was a great distraction from the whole pandemic situation. I was being really careful during these runs (and in general), trying to stay two metres apart from those who I jogged past on the pavements.

I did the St Albans 10k in April with Adam. This was one of the first running events to go ahead as restrictions slowly eased. It felt a bit like a parkrun, and I loved it. Not having parkrun around was really difficult, and I was missing that social side of running.

At this point, I was still going to Man On! football sessions, and I was starting to realise that I would not be able to carry on doing this without getting injured. But I found a temporary solution and decided to play in goal only, which took some getting used to – and plenty of blunders!

However, it still became obvious that marathon training was going to take over my spare time, and sacrifices would have to be made. This was hard to get used to and sometimes took the fun and enjoyment out of running, but I had made a commitment and was determined to see it through.

By the end of May, I had my second vaccine, and things were starting to look better as summer approached. For a start, the cinema was back open, and I was delighted to get back to my happy place!

I also enjoyed watching England get to the Euro 2020 final, and, despite the heart-breaking ending, it provided a lot of happy memories watching the wins with friends and family.

The only thing that was nagging at me around this time was work. I was still enjoying the role, but it became clear it was never going to become anything more senior, and I didn't want my job title to be "assistant" for the rest of my days.

I had a few unsuccessful interviews, but then in July a role came up that was just perfect. A local charity, Hertfordshire Mind Network, was looking for a marketing officer, so I applied straight away. I had really wanted to work in mental health for so long, and this was a wonderful opportunity. One of my previous interviews was actually with the national Mind charity based in Stratford, London. In hindsight, I don't think I would have enjoyed the long commute into central London, so probably best I didn't get that one.

I was out doing one of my training runs when I got the call from Herts Mind Network offering me the job. I had a massive spring in my step for the rest of that run! I had finally achieved something that I had really wanted for the last few years: a job in mental health that not only helped other people, but where I could use my degree, skills, experience and passion. This was a huge deal.

It was perfect timing as well. The following week, Holly and I were heading to Gibraltar for the wedding of one of my mates (also called James) from uni – time to celebrate! I didn't actually decide to share the news just yet, since I only had the offer verbally and hadn't signed a contract. I didn't want to jinx it or anything.

That trip was easily one of the highlights of 2021. It was amazing to forget about the last year or so and how hard the pandemic had made life. The wedding took place on a yacht called Sunborn, and it was spectacular. We spent a long weekend in the company of best friends, in warm sunshine and swimming pools, with good food and drinks. It's a shame we were only away a few nights – we did not want it to end! In addition to the wedding, we tried to do as many activities as possible in Gibraltar. The stand-out was going up to the huge rock and seeing the local apes, although they were very pesky little buggers!

# SOCIAL MEDIA AND MENTAL HEALTH

It's a shame that, these days, social media can be associated with toxicity and trolls. I really like it and have since it started. I even based my final year project and master's dissertation on it, as I have always found it really fascinating. I still enjoy using it now – although I am aware I probably post and share too much! I think one of the reasons why I am fond of it is because I make sure my feeds only contain people who post content that I like, and I am a big fan of hitting either the unfollow or mute buttons. I believe it's important to do this so that you get the best experience out of it, otherwise it could end up having a negative effect on your mental health, as it did with me in the lead-up to my first psychotic episode.

These are some of the accounts I follow that I would also recommend for keeping your socials full of goodness:

Instagram:
- @Mattzhaig
- @thebodycoach (Joe Wicks)
- @BrittPfluger
- @BeUrOwnLightBlog
- @TriggerHub_
- @MrJonnyBenjamin
- @WeAreBey0nd
- @MindCharity
- @MHBlogAwards

Twitter:
- @MoveWellness21
- @PowerofLetters1

# CHAPTER 24

# LIFE IS A MARATHON, NOT A SPRINT

In September 2021, I was lucky enough to get another chance to go on a podcast. This happened through Twitter. An account for the *Inside the Orange* podcast followed me, and I decided to follow back, as it looked really interesting. Earlier in the year, they had put out a tweet saying that they were looking for new people to interview for season three. I messaged them privately saying I would be happy to take part, and I let them know what topics I could cover (including mental health).

It turned out that the man behind the pod (Richard) was also from Watford and was a huge Watford FC fan too, so we had plenty in common. The recording was really positive, and we had lots to chat about; mainly football, running and mental health. I was able to give a shout out to Watford CSE Trust for their great work with Man On!, and I mentioned my upcoming marathon and my history with Mind, as well as my current job. I really enjoy taking part in things like this, and the episode was really well received – it got great feedback from my friends, family and colleagues. I would not hesitate to do something similar again, providing I am in the right health and coping with my workload – I have learnt the hard way not to over-do it!

That same month, three of my uni friends and I managed to go abroad for a short trip to Slovenia. This included one of the most fun things I have ever done so far in my life. We booked a canyoning experience, which I found exhilarating, and I was so happy we did this. It is definitely up there with my other bucket list things (right next to skydiving when I was 18).

This holiday was also my first experience of driving abroad, which took some getting used to! Another highlight was the day we hired e-bikes and cycled around Lake Bled. We even stopped and swam in the lake for a bit – an awesome experience all round.

When I got home, I was pleasantly surprised to be contacted by someone from a company called Pitney Bowes Ltd. He explained that he and his colleagues were taking part in The Prince's Trust Million Makers, a challenge through which they were aiming to raise over £10,000 for the charity. To do this, they were putting together an inspirational book of stories called *The Power of Letters* and asked if I would be willing to write a letter for the book. Of course, I was more than happy to take part! I sent them a letter about my mental illness journey so far, and they added it to their website. The actual book was released in 2022, and my letter was included in there too! Here is a shortened version of it.

# A MESSAGE OF HOPE, FROM YOUR PAL

Dear friend,

I hope that as you are reading this you are in a place of happiness, but if not, that is okay. You are not alone and you never will be.

Things might be far from perfect, but always remember that you are enough. A few years ago I was in a very dark and sad place. I went through the scariest and most difficult period of my life.

Thankfully I am now over the worst of it and am currently living a much happier life. The reason I am telling you these things is because I want you to know that even if you hit rock bottom, you can turn it around. The thing with rock bottom is that you discover the solid, unbreakable, courageous part of yourself that will never be beaten, and you can build on that foundation and make it even better than it once was. You might be hitting the reset button, maybe more than once, but trust me, you will build something to be proud of.

Life can be hard, but life is also very precious. Try and surround yourself with people who make you happy and make you laugh out loud.

I do not regret becoming mentally ill, because it took me on a journey that has eventually transformed me into the best version of myself.

Self-care and self-awareness are so important. If you think you need help, always seek it. If you think you can help someone else, be there for them – it might even save their life.

Try not to compare yourself to others. We are all so beautifully unique as individuals, and your journey is completely different to everyone else's. Embrace your imperfections, your weirdness, your everything.

Try not to be hard on yourself – you are not your thoughts. It might feel like your mind is a storm at times, but this will pass, and the sunshine is closer than you think.

I hope you have found my little letter helpful, wherever you are.

Thanks for reading, and thanks for being you.

James, 31, from Hertfordshire

Back to the big day in London – the marathon had arrived. I was starting to get nervous, and I had a bit of a thigh/quad/hip flexor injury scare a few weeks before the race. Thankfully I was still able to cross the finish line on the actual day, and it was magnificent – probably my favourite run of all time. The atmosphere in the city was incredible, and I was boosted by having Holly, Mum and some friends cheering me on.

We had to get up really early to hop on the train into London and go to the start line. I was a mixture of excited and nervous, as I was about to run further than I had ever ran. I began the run at a very slow pace, as I was very mindful of my injury. Then, as I was getting close to the halfway point, I realised that my leg was not giving me too much pain, so I began to jog at normal pace and started to enjoy the occasion more.

Around 13 miles into the race, I crossed Tower Bridge, and this is where I saw some friends in the crowd. Then, not long after, I spotted Holly and Mum as well. I cannot emphasise enough how much difference it makes seeing your loved ones during a marathon. It had such a good psychological effect on me and gave me thoughts like, "I can do this, I am actually going to do this!"

Running a marathon is just as much of a mental battle as it is physical. The second half was so brutal, and I was glad I had a Spotify playlist in my ears to keep me going. People in the crowd give out water, energy drinks, sweets and fruit throughout the course, which also helps massively.

I will never forget the sheer joy and elation of crossing the finish line. I was also so relieved to bring to an end such a difficult year of training, but it is definitely one of my proudest achievements.

I think what I mean by the chapter title is this: before I got sectioned, I was chasing all my life goals like a sprinter. I was so keen to have a successful career and relationships that I was rushing it and wanted everything right away.

Nowadays, I have accepted that I will hopefully do all the things I want at some point, but I need to approach life at a steady jogging pace. Everyone has their own journey, and there is no point in being fixated on achieving something within a timeframe.

Holly and I have gone through the stressful process of buying our own flat too, which was very exciting and worth it when it all finally went through! The saga of getting it completed definitely took it out of me mentally at times. It got frustrating having to call the solicitor and estate agent every week, especially when the sale kept getting delayed. Moving all our stuff was hard too, and unfortunately the seller left the flat in a bit of a dirty state. At one point, Mum did admit she was worried about me, as I was letting it stress me out fairly often. Thankfully, once we were moved and settled, things were much better.

We are now living in a lovely two-bedroom flat in west Watford, a great location not far from the town centre, and pretty close to the football stadium too – win! It only takes me around 15 minutes to drive to work, or 20 or so minutes if I decide to cycle. The flat is not far away from Cassiobury Park too, where my local parkrun happens (another win). We live really close to Holly's parents, and about a ten-minute drive from my parents and Mark, so we have plenty of chances to see them for dinner and things like that.

Things were really looking up, and I can safely say I was in a good place by this point. It had sometimes been a bit of a rollercoaster, but I had accepted mental illness will always be a part of me. I was no longer ashamed to have schizoaffective disorder, and I decided to start to befriend it, rather than hide from it. My medication was and is 200mg of quetiapine per day, and it works out for me, mainly because it allows me to fall asleep every night without much struggling, and it helps prevent me from having racing thoughts. I can't imagine not being on the meds, and I am fine with that. I have forgotten to take them until just before bed on the odd occasion – I am supposed to take them around dinner time – and it really shows. Without their effects, I feel my mind racing in bed, so I am thankful they prevent that.

In February 2022, I raised £345 for Hertfordshire Mind Network by running the Watford Half Marathon. This was another proud occasion, and I was happy to get another medal, but also felt that this should be my last long run for the time being. The route was very hilly, enough to put anyone off running!

In March, I had one of the most humbling experiences ever when a school group and their teacher reached out to me on Twitter about my first Mind blog. They were an A-Level drama group based in Southampton, and wanted to do a Zoom call with me asking questions about my psychosis experience. The call was just so fulfilling because I could tell it meant a lot to them to have a real-life case study. Their questions were so well prepared and really thought-provoking. I was happy to have helped them on their project.

I had a similar experience the same month when a university student reached out to us at work. She wanted to interview men who have had experience with group counselling as part of her dissertation. Taking part in this was hugely rewarding as well. I try my best to give back when things like this come up because I remember being at school and at university, and I know getting participants for research is not always easy, but when you do, their contributions are invaluable.

Also in early 2022, my job title changed to Fundraising & Marketing Officer. I saw the chance to take on some fundraising tasks and decided to take them on to make my role more varied, and also to add another string to my bow in terms of my CV and progressing up the career ladder. This job change led to getting involved in loads more things. Some were more challenging than others, but I had decided my attitude was going to be "challenge accepted".

# MENTAL HEALTH QUOTES

Quotes are wonderful things, and they have the power to turn our days around, inspire us, make us more determined, and much more. I've made a list here of my favourites that have helped me over the years:

- *"Life begins at the edge of your comfort zone"* – **Neale Donald Walsch** (my personal favourite quote)

- *"Mental health problems don't define who you are. They are something you experience. You walk in the rain and you feel the rain, but you are not the rain."* – **Matt Haig**

- *"The experience I have had is that once you start talking about [experiencing a mental health struggle], you realise that actually you're part of quite a big club."* – **Prince Harry**

- *"Promise me you'll always remember: you're braver than you believe, and stronger than you seem, and smarter than you think."* – **Christopher Robin from *Winnie the Pooh***

- *"If you have been brutally broken but still have the courage to be gentle to other living beings, then you're a badass with a heart of an angel."* – **Keanu Reeves**

- *"The way I see it, if you want to see the rainbow, you've got to put up with the rain."* – **Dolly Parton**

- *"Nothing is impossible. The word itself says, 'I'm possible!'"* 
  – **Audrey Hepburn**

- *"You have to be where you are to get where you need to go."* 
  – **Amy Poehler**

- *"Being vulnerable is a strength, not a weakness."* – **Selena Gomez**

- *"No matter what you're going through, there's a light at the end of the tunnel."* – **Demi Lovato**

- *"Recovery needs a much broader definition than just reduction in symptoms. I see recovery as the restoration of self-esteem, meaning, quality of life and moments of joy."* – **Victoria Maxwell**

- *"Always live your life to the fullest like it's a never-ending parade. Fill it with every kind of colour and music that has you dancing amongst strangers as though they were lifelong friends."* – **James McInerney**

- *"The comeback is always stronger than the setback."* – **Catherine Plano**

# CHAPTER 25

# JOINING THE FIGHT FOR MENTAL HEALTH

I am now where I feel I belong career-wise, working for a mental health charity. It is massively satisfying to help people for a living, and I hope I can do plenty of great things at Herts Mind Network.

I've not always been the best at giving presentations and speaking in front of groups of people, but when the cause is close to my heart, I am able to rise to the challenge and provide a performance level that I wasn't able to reach before. It's a little out of my comfort zone at times, but it is pushing me and making me more resilient, which I think is a positive thing. So far in this job, I have given a lot of presentations, some of them very last minute. They can make me a bit anxious, but when they are over, I get such a buzz and sometimes even feel a bit euphoric.

I think it helps having lived experience of mental illness, as it makes the presentation a lot more authentic for the people watching. I can tell they appreciate it when I am open and honest about what I have been through.

The majority of my days working for a local Mind charity have been fantastic, but there are some days that are challenging when I am exposed to the lives of local residents and their mental illnesses.

One time, I had a chance to take on a different type of responsibility by becoming one of our "safeguarding champions". One person from each department was going to get extra training, and this group would meet monthly to go through all things safeguarding. This seemed okay at first, even if it was completely different to my day job. Then I realised I felt quite out of my depth, as all the other champions were in roles where they dealt with the mentally unwell pretty much every day. I have so much respect for my colleagues because they help people with all sorts of terrible problems such as domestic abuse, homelessness and suicidal intentions.

The next time I went to the champions meeting, I remember we were going through a list of recent safeguarding issues and discussing how they were dealt with, or, if applicable, how they could have been handled better. I found this particular meeting quite difficult because all of the cases we went through were people who had been trying to take their own lives. It really hit home that a lot of people living in Hertfordshire were suicidal, which I found heart-breaking and really upsetting. It made me realise how important we were as a charity, and I tried not to dwell on the negative, but rather tried to focus on how many people we were saving from themselves by making their lives worth living.

I decided after that meeting to step away from the champion role. I wasn't ready to be exposed to that much mental illness. I knew that getting too involved with others can sometimes put your own health at risk. I was also really busy with my own workload, so I didn't want to overwhelm myself mentally or emotionally. It was useful experience, and I could maybe do it another time, but I had to put my own well-being first and be mindful of my stress levels.

Speaking of stress, the month of April is an important month in our work calendar, as it is Stress Awareness Month. I emailed the rest of the charity asking what things help them with stress, and I received loads of great tips that I was able to put out as great content on our social media channels.

I got the chance to make my own contribution to the month outside of work, when I had the chance to write a blog for Cherish Editions, the mental health publisher behind this book. This one was about my own personal stress-busters.

# STRESS AWARENESS MONTH: 8 TIPS TO TRY WHEN YOU'RE STRESSED

I want to share with you what I've learnt about maintaining good mental well-being. I must first point out that these tips are what work for me personally. They may also work for you, but everyone is different – it's important to figure out what is effective for you, as well as the things you should avoid.

### 1. Be Active
Firstly, I am a massive advocate for all things sport and exercise. Fitness can take many forms, and there are so many things you can try. I personally think stepping out of your comfort zone is worth it too, even if it's just a small departure.

### 2. Talk It Out
I think having an outlet is so important for relieving stress. It's important to keep talking to each other, whether you do so with family, friends, teammates or mental health professionals. Most of the time, when you tell someone else what is stressing you out, the admission alone gives you so much relief.

### 3. Feed Your Mind
Something I wish I'd discovered sooner is that what we eat and drink has a massive impact on our stress levels.

I find that I feel better when I stick to meals that have high protein and plenty of vegetables. There is a lot of information out there on stress and nutrition.

### 4. Be Present
I am gutted that I only started doing meditation in my mid-20s. This technique does wonders for me, and it would have made school and university a smoother experience.

There are plenty of useful apps to help you do this – I have found Headspace and Calm to be very effective. Try doing a short meditation at different times of day and see what the difference is.

### 5. Get Creative
Have you ever tried writing as a form of therapy? I find it to be a really comforting experience – even writing this blog is putting me in a great mood! There are also some fantastic adult colouring books out there now. Order one online – you won't regret it!

### 6. Gaming
This one isn't for everyone, but I find that when I play certain games on my PlayStation, it really zones me out and almost resets my mind. I guess because it's a form of escapism, I immerse myself in it, and it often calms me as a result.

### 7. Get Lost in a Movie
Speaking of escapism, I have an unlimited cinema membership, and I can tell you right now that it is one of my favourite things to do. I am even happy to go on my own because it's some of the best "me time" I can have. I love being away from my phone for two hours and completely throwing myself into the story on the big screen.

### 8. Face Your Fears
Lastly, I want to mention something that really stuck with me when I was having CBT (cognitive behavioural therapy) sessions a few years ago. Sometimes, our natural instinct is to avoid or run away from stress and uncertainly. However, a better option may be to embrace it, befriend it and learn how to cope with it.

I loved the feeling of getting another blog published online, and it led to some great chats with colleagues at work who read it. I was also making an effort to connect with other writers and bloggers online, and it wasn't long before the next opportunity presented itself.

# CHAPTER 26

# AT PEACE WITH MY MENTAL ILLNESS

By this point, I was quite at peace with having schizoaffective disorder and I even wanted to write about it. I had not seen a great deal of coverage on my condition and I was keen to put something out there, as well as hopefully learning more about it myself. I had discovered there were some Facebook groups about it, which had thousands of members from all over the world, so I joined these and would regularly see new updates.

I was also discovering that working in mental health was turning out to be some of the most fulfilling work I have ever done. Every time I gave a presentation or talk, I would always mention my own lived experience, and this seemed to help a lot, both for me and the audience.

In April, we were contacted by a lady called Sophie who produces a podcast called *Hemel Talk*. They cover the local community in Hemel Hempstead and shine a spotlight on charities and organisations. They wanted to do an episode with us and release it during Mental Health Awareness Week in May.

I was happy to be part of this and was one of three Herts Mind Network staff who spoke to Sophie about our charity. It was really nice to tell her about the great work we were doing in Hemel, as well as the rest of Hertfordshire. I briefly mentioned my mental illness, and that led to her asking plenty of follow-up questions, so my bit included some personal parts as well, which I didn't mind at all.

Another work project that I am really proud of is our support for refugees. It was around this time that the dreadful Russo-Ukrainian

War was happening, which was both scary and heart-breaking. A few months earlier I had seen a grant opportunity for charities who were supporting refugees. We had already been trying to start a weekly support group for those affected by the Russo-Ukrainian War, so I sent this opportunity to our chief executive, and she ended up applying. Then, I was delighted to hear that we were successful, and we were going to be starting a weekly group dedicated to Ukrainian refugees in Hertfordshire. I ended up going along to the first group, and it was quite emotional. One lady that showed up was very distraught and tearful because she didn't know if her sister was alive. Her young nephew was also still in Ukraine fighting, and her niece was apparently stuck in Romania. I felt so heartbroken for her, but there were a few people in the group who were giving her some really good practical advice, such as who to contact and how to apply for a visa. The emotion of that day stuck with me, and I felt proud that we were making a difference. The experience put things in perspective for me too. My daily concerns were around painting our flat and getting holidays sorted; these refugees were literally going through hell, and I felt so lucky to have the life that I had.

I saw another chance to produce a blog when I started chatting to Eleanor Segall (author and regular blogger – check out beurownlight.com for her brilliant work). I mentioned that I would be keen to make a contribution, and she was very happy for me to do it. I decided to make this one more about my schizoaffective disorder since, up until this point, I had not really covered it in my other blogs. Eleanor published it on 9 May 2022 – the first day of Mental Health Awareness Week – so I was happy to be able to contribute during such an important time. You can read the post on Eleanor's website; I've shared the link at the back of this book.

I emailed that blog to my colleagues and had plenty of heart-warming feedback from them, which also led to some nice conversations around the topic. Later that same week, the podcast episode from *Hemel Talk* was released, which also went down very well and gave me a lot of job satisfaction.

I am open to doing more media work like this, and I am looking forward to hopefully more opportunities coming along.

# A LETTER TO MY PAST SELF –
# FROM 2022 ME TO 2017 ME

Dear friend,

It's me (you) from the future, five years from now.

Firstly, I am really sorry for the way things are at the moment. I know that you are feeling the saddest and most depressed that you've ever felt in your whole life. You feel like giving up, and even though you are not quite suicidal, you appreciate how suicidal people feel because you really hate your life right now. You go to bed dreading the next day, then in the morning you stay in bed because there is nothing worth getting up for. You feel at an all-time low, like you have hit rock bottom. You beat yourself up because you think breaking up with Ellie was the biggest mistake of all time. You miss her and the life you had, the person you were. But I can tell you with the benefit of my hindsight, you were incredibly brave to end the relationship because you were living a lie. It also sucked that you lost your job, but let's be honest, you hated that job anyway. You need to put fulfilment first and get a new role that you are passionate about.

I know you won't believe me when I say this, but you ARE going to bounce back, and you are going to find happiness again.

Your psychotic episode was traumatic, but think of it as a thing that had to happen. Think of it as the reset button, hitting refresh, wiping the slate clean. You broke down, but you can build yourself back up and become even better. You're going to become James 2.0, a better version of yourself.

You still have plenty to learn, but we both know you're a great learner – otherwise, you wouldn't have a master's degree, would you?!

Trust me, you need to start prioritising your mental health. I know it's hard, but you also need to face what happened to you and learn from it.

So, where to start? Well, first you need to get your medication right. Aripiprazole keeps our condition at bay, but it's far too sedating. Don't come off meds (trust me, I found out the hard way), but find better meds that don't suck your energy and life force away. I would also recommend getting some therapy – you've been through so much shit, and you need to process it all.

Once you've done that, do a bit more exercise and try a bit of a healthier diet, you will be surprised how good this will make you feel.

Plus, I know you're ashamed of your situation right now, but be more sociable and get out there more. Wallowing in your sadness is not the best way to spend your 20s – live in the moment. See your friends as much as you can, it will do you a world of good.

Lastly, I know you think you won't be lucky enough to find a relationship like Ellie again, but I am going to give you a spoiler here because once you start finding happiness within yourself, the girl will come. Everything that you want is achievable and more – it's all waiting for you to go out and get it. I am so massively proud of you, dude – I could cry right now.

Promise me (and yourself) that you will keep going. Don't just do it for yourself – do it for the person you are going to become (this guy!), because I am looking back at you right now with immense admiration. You've got this!!

Yours sincerely, your older (slightly balder) self xx

# CHAPTER 27

# ONWARDS AND UPWARDS

I think this feels the right time to bring this particular story to an end.

I've got plenty of plans and ambitions for the future. Holly and I want to get married and have kids. We want to see as much of the world as we can. She would like to take me to India, where her grandpa is from, which I am really keen to do! I would love to progress at work. I like the idea of reaching manager level if I can, and hopefully I will be able to handle it.

My life goals have not changed a lot since encountering mental illness all those years ago, but my attitude has changed a great deal (for the better). I no longer put enormous pressure on myself. I spend a lot less time comparing myself to others. I am kinder to myself, and I try my best to always live in the moment.

I am eager to do more for mental health. Psychosis is the worst thing that has happened to me, and I would not wish it on my worst enemy. It is good to talk and share, and I am glad I was able to start doing this. I am pleased that my job enables me to help people, and long may that continue.

Thank you so, so much for reading! I started writing this to help myself, but also to help others, so if this transcript provides comfort to even one person, then it will be worth it, and I will be more than satisfied.

I highly encourage writing about mental health, or any other form of sharing – podcasting, videos, open conversations with people, etc. If you feel comfortable doing so, I have found it so therapeutic and such a healthy escape at times. It is helpful for processing and understanding your thoughts, and in my case, for befriending my mental illness and being at peace with it. However, I would also say that it is definitely something that needs to be done at your own pace and within your comfort zone, where possible. It's important to keep in mind that anything that involves thinking back to a mental illness experience can be traumatic and even triggering. If you feel ready to take that first step, I would say go for it! You will not know until you try, and I bet you won't regret it. ☺

# PRAISE FOR *BEFRIENDING MY BRAIN*

*Befriending My Brain* is a brilliant must-read. I found it impossible to put down once I started it. James' journey with his mental health is extremely compelling, insightful, and, ultimately, **inspirational**.

This book offers a beacon of hope to anyone who may be struggling with mental illness, as well as their loved ones. James is the true personification of the concept that there is always *"light at the end of the tunnel."*

—Jonny Benjamin MBE, mental health advocate and author of *The Stranger on the Bridge*

# ACKNOWLEDGEMENTS

There are so many people who made this possible that I want to thank. Firstly, I must mention Mum, who not only never gave up on me when I became unwell, but maybe even more importantly, she was the reason I never gave up on myself. My dad and my brother Mark have also been incredibly supportive, understanding and caring.

I wouldn't be the person I am without my friends, who did and continue to do so much to inspire me and always have my back. Thank you for the amazing things you did when I got ill, contacting my mum, keeping each other in the loop, but also picking me up when I was down and being the reason that I have so many incredible life memories and adventures.

Thank you to my colleagues past and present, who were so accommodating and flexible with my mental illness, made me feel valued and heard, and were always willing to help in any way they could and can. You create the work environment I need and make it impossible for me to ever have Sunday blues.

Lastly, I want to give an enormous thank you to Holly. After I was sectioned, I truly believed I would never be lucky enough to meet and fall in love with someone as wonderful as you. When I relapsed not long after we met, you stuck with me despite how hard things were. You always believe in me and make me feel like I can do anything with you by my side. You make me laugh out loud every day, and I am one extremely lucky dude! I love you so much.

# ABOUT THE AUTHOR

James is 32 and lives with his partner Holly in Watford, Hertfordshire. He currently enjoys working in marketing for Hertfordshire Mind Network, his local mental health charity. In his spare time, he likes to play football, go to the cinema, hang out with friends and family, and explore exciting new places with Holly.

James also likes to get involved with mental health causes in any way he can to help others, raise awareness and reduce stigma. So far, he has blogged online extensively, spoken on several podcasts, and appeared on TV and video for the Premier League in 2019, as well as for McLaren in 2022.

You can keep up with James on Twitter @JamesLindsay23.

# BLOGS BY JAMES LINDSAY

- **I Joined #TeamMind After Running Transformed My Mental Health**
  - https://www.mind.org.uk/information-support/your-stories/i-joined-teammind-after-running-transformed-my-mental-health/

- **Alumni Stories: James Lindsay and Coping with Mental Health During Covid-19**
  - http://blogs.herts.ac.uk/2020/04/alumni-stories-james-lindsay-and-coping.html

- **How Football Has Helped Me Through Relapses and Covid-19**
  - https://www.mind.org.uk/information-support/your-stories/how-football-has-helped-me-through-relapses-and-covid19/

- **A Message of Hope, From Your Pal**
  - https://www.thepowerofletters.com/copy-of-if-only-i-knew-1

- **Stress Awareness Month: 8 Tips to Try When You're Stressed**
  - https://cherisheditions.com/2022/04/11/stress-awareness-month-8-tips-to-try/

- **Learning to Accept and Embrace Having Schizoaffective Disorder This Mental Health Awareness Week**
  - https://beurownlight.com/2022/05/09/learning-to-accept-and-embrace-having-schizoaffective-disorder-this-mental-health-awareness-week-by-james-lindsay/

# ABOUT CHERISH EDITIONS

Cherish Editions is a bespoke self-publishing service for authors of mental health, well-being and inspirational books.

As a division of Trigger Publishing, the UK's leading independent mental health and well-being publisher, we are experienced in creating and selling positive, responsible, important and inspirational books, which work to de-stigmatize the issues around mental health and improve the mental health and well-being of those who read our titles.

Founded by Adam Shaw, a mental health advocate, author and philanthropist, and leading psychologist Lauren Callaghan, Cherish Editions aims to publish books that provide advice, support and inspiration. We nurture our authors so that their stories can unfurl on the page, helping them to share their uplifting and moving stories.

Cherish Editions is unique in that a percentage of the profits from the sale of our books goes directly to leading mental health charity Shawmind, to deliver its vision to provide support for those experiencing mental ill health.

Find out more about Cherish Editions by visiting cherisheditions.com or joining us on:
    Twitter @cherisheditions
    Facebook @cherisheditions
    Instagram @cherisheditions

Cherish
EDITIONS

# ABOUT SHAWMIND

A proportion of profits from the sale of all Trigger books go to their sister charity, Shawmind, also founded by Adam Shaw and Lauren Callaghan. The charity aims to ensure that everyone has access to mental health resources whenever they need them.

Find out more about the work Shawmind do by visiting shawmind.org or joining them on:

Twitter @Shawmind_
Facebook @ShawmindUK
Instagram @Shawmind_

Your Local Mental Health & Wellbeing Charity

Lightning Source UK Ltd.
Milton Keynes UK
UKHW042209230223
417529UK00004B/94

9 781913 615949